Building a 3D Game with LibGDX

Learn how to build an exciting 3D game with LibGDX from scratch

Sebastián Di Giuseppe

Andreas Krühlmann

Elmar van Rijnswou

BIRMINGHAM - MUMBAI

Building a 3D Game with LibGDX

First published: August 2016

Production reference: 1220816

Published by Packt Publishing Ltd.
Livery Place
35 Livery Street
Birmingham
B3 2PB, UK.
ISBN 978-1-78528-841-8

www.packtpub.com

Credits

Authors

Sebastián Di Giuseppe

Andreas Krühlmann

Elmar van Rijnswou

Reviewer

Jean-Baptiste Simillon

Commissioning Editor

Amarabha Banerjee

Acquisition Editor

Aaron Lazar

Content Development Editor

Anish Sukumaran

Technical Editor

Kunal Chaudhari

Copy Editor

Zainab Bootwala

Project Coordinator

Izzat Contractor

Proofreader

Safis Editing

Indexer

Tejal Daruwale Soni

Graphics

Abhinash Sahu

Production Coordinator

Aparna Bhagat

About the Author

Sebastian Di Giuseppe started back in 2011 with Java game development and native Android development. With a huge passion, he spent a lot of time learning the different areas of game development, exploring programming areas, and creating prototypes of all kinds for several platforms. With a good plan for his improvement while having a full time job as an Android developer, he also spends a lot of time on the forum, `java-gaming.org`, learning and making contacts. He joined forces with a graphic designer and a musician to peruse more professional tasks and updates on their work that led him to meet a team of developers who called themselves Deeep Games. With them, he took a step up and also learned project and product management. With time, he joined and consulted other game development teams on management and processes. He now works as a full-time project and product manager and you can see him hang out on the *Indie Game Developers'* Facebook group posting updates on prototypes, ideas, or recruiting for future projects. You check out his LinkedIn profile at `https://ar.linkedin.com/in/sebadigiuseppe` or his Facebook profile at `https://www.facebook.com/sebastian.digiuseppe.54`.

I'd like to thank, Elmar Van Rijnswou and Andreas Krülmann for inviting me to join Deeep Games, which was a huge boost to my career. Packt Publishing, along with Aaron Lazar and Anish Sukumaran take a huge gratitude from me for being so patient, helpful, and supportive on the project, and for giving me this huge opportunity. Also, thanks to Oliver Mendoza for helping synthesize an easy and representative 3D model development along with its other areas.

www.PacktPub.com

eBooks, discount offers, and more

Did you know that Packt offers eBook versions of every book published, with PDF and ePub files available? You can upgrade to the eBook version at www.PacktPub.com and as a print book customer, you are entitled to a discount on the eBook copy. Get in touch with us at customercare@packtpub.com for more details.

At www.PacktPub.com, you can also read a collection of free technical articles, sign up for a range of free newsletters and receive exclusive discounts and offers on Packt books and eBooks.

https://www2.packtpub.com/books/subscription/packtlib

Do you need instant solutions to your IT questions? PacktLib is Packt's online digital book library. Here, you can search, access, and read Packt's entire library of books.

Why subscribe?

- Fully searchable across every book published by Packt
- Copy and paste, print, and bookmark content
- On demand and accessible via a web browser

Table of Contents

Preface

Building a 3D Game with LibGDX is a book about how to create games with LibGDX that can work in 3D. We'll cover camera differences with 2D primitive shapes, a game design "on the run" approach, modeling our assets, getting assets from websites, preparing our models and downloading them to be used with LibGDX, animations, textures, a basic UI and with Tweening, all toward developing a basic FPS game. And finally, we will get to export to a desired platform along with troubleshooting usual problems.

What this book covers

Chapter 1, *Setting Up Your Development Environment*, will cover everything we need to install in order to have a workflow.

Chapter 2, *An Extra Dimension*, will go over the differences between a 2D and a 3D camera, and then set up a base to work with and draw primitive shapes.

Chapter 3, *Working toward a Prototype*, will go over the creation of a prototype, from the creation of a level with enemies, chase mechanics, physics, collisions, a user interface, and a mechanism to defend ourselves from the enemies.

Chapter 4, *Preparing Visuals*, will walk us through the basics of how to use Blender and go step by step through how to create a representative model for our game.

Chapter 5, *Starting to Look Like an Actual Game*, will help you prepare and import the model created in the previous chapter as well as from other sources. We will also get collision shapes from a static model and add basic shadows.

Chapter 6, *Spicing Up the Game*, will help you polish your game a little by adding a particle system and some UI Tweening. You will also work a bit on the performance of the game and explore the .NET API, brought by LibGDX, by adding online Leaderboards.

Chapter 7, *Final Words*, will demonstrate deploying games on various platforms and some basic troubleshooting. This chapter will also help you identify the platform we are running the game on, and finally, talk about room for improvement.

What you need for this book

For this book we'll need the following:

- Intellij IDEA Community Edition, at least version 14.1.4
- LibGDX's Setup App, at least version 1.6.4
- Java JDK
- Android SDK with at least API 22

Who this book is for

If you are a game developer or an enthusiast who wants to build 3D games with LibGDX, then this book is for you. Some basic knowledge of LibGDX and Java programming is required.

Conventions

In this book, you will find a number of text styles that distinguish between different kinds of information. Here are some examples of these styles and an explanation of their meaning.

Code words in text, database table names, folder names, filenames, file extensions, pathnames, dummy URLs, user input, and Twitter handles are shown as follows: "The AddScore(..) will do the obvious: reading our Strings for the high scores."

A block of code is set as follows:

```
public static final float VIRTUAL_HEIGHT = 540;
Screen screen;
@Override
    public void create() {
        Gdx.input.setCatchBackKey(true);
        setScreen(new GameScreen(this));
```

Any command-line input or output is written as follows:

```
fbx-conv-win32.exe -f -v myModel.fbx convertedModel.g3db
```

New terms and **important words** are shown in bold. Words that you see on the screen, for example, in menus or dialog boxes, appear in the text like this: "Click on **Generate** and wait. After it is done, open IntelliJ IDEA "

Warnings or important notes appear in a box like this.

 Tips and tricks appear like this.

Reader feedback

Feedback from our readers is always welcome. Let us know what you think about this book-what you liked or disliked. Reader feedback is important for us as it helps us develop titles that you will really get the most out of. To send us general feedback, simply e-mail feedback@packtpub.com, and mention the book's title in the subject of your message. If there is a topic that you have expertise in and you are interested in either writing or contributing to a book, see our author guide at www.packtpub.com/authors.

Customer support

Now that you are the proud owner of a Packt book, we have a number of things to help you to get the most from your purchase.

Downloading the example code

You can download the example code files for this book from your account at http://www.packtpub.com. If you purchased this book elsewhere, you can visit http://www.packtpub.com/support and register to have the files e-mailed directly to you.

You can download the code files by following these steps:

1. Log in or register to our website using your e-mail address and password.
2. Hover the mouse pointer on the **SUPPORT** tab at the top.
3. Click on **Code Downloads & Errata**.
4. Enter the name of the book in the **Search** box.
5. Select the book for which you're looking to download the code files.
6. Choose from the drop-down menu where you purchased this book from.
7. Click on **Code Download**.

Once the file is downloaded, please make sure that you unzip or extract the folder using the latest version of:

- WinRAR / 7-Zip for Windows
- Zipeg / iZip / UnRarX for Mac
- 7-Zip / PeaZip for Linux

The code bundle for the book is also hosted on GitHub at https://github.com/PacktPubl ishing/Buildinga3DGamewithLibGDX. We also have other code bundles from our rich catalog of books and videos available at https://github.com/PacktPublishing/. Check them out!

Downloading the color images of this book

We also provide you with a PDF file that has color images of the screenshots/diagrams used in this book. The color images will help you better understand the changes in the output. You can download this file from http://www.packtpub.com/sites/default/files/downl oads/Buildinga3DGamewithLibGDX_ColorImages.pdf.

Errata

Although we have taken every care to ensure the accuracy of our content, mistakes do happen. If you find a mistake in one of our books-maybe a mistake in the text or the code-we would be grateful if you could report this to us. By doing so, you can save other readers from frustration and help us improve subsequent versions of this book. If you find any errata, please report them by visiting http://www.packtpub.com/submit-errata, selecting your book, clicking on the **Errata Submission Form** link, and entering the details of your errata. Once your errata are verified, your submission will be accepted and the errata will be uploaded to our website or added to any list of existing errata under the Errata section of that title.

To view the previously submitted errata, go to https://www.packtpub.com/books/conten t/support and enter the name of the book in the search field. The required information will appear under the **Errata** section.

Piracy

Piracy of copyrighted material on the Internet is an ongoing problem across all media. At Packt, we take the protection of our copyright and licenses very seriously. If you come across any illegal copies of our works in any form on the Internet, please provide us with the location address or website name immediately so that we can pursue a remedy.

Please contact us at copyright@packtpub.com with a link to the suspected pirated material.

We appreciate your help in protecting our authors and our ability to bring you valuable content.

Questions

If you have a problem with any aspect of this book, you can contact us at questions@packtpub.com, and we will do our best to address the problem.

1
Setting Up Your Development Environment

LibGDX's development is very powerful, and that is why we will set up a nice and stable structure to work with before jumping into the code and project structure. We will use IntelliJ IDEA to do most of our development for the simply because it's productive (and of course, there are few neat tricks to combine with LibGDX), though it's very common to use Eclipse for development too. There are other ways to set up a 3D game with LibGDX, but to start off this book; we will build the game with basic assets created by code. In this chapter, we will explain how to download and set up all the required tools to get you started with setting up an environment to build 3D games with LibGDX, and to work on desktop and Android platforms. Although LibGDX also builds for HTML (WebGL) and iOS, we won't cover these builds because they do not fit with our game, but they are as easy as the following documentation guidelines on the official site (`http://libgdx.badlogicgames.com/`). You will learn more about this in this chapter.

Assuming you know LibGDX, you already have the **Java Development Kit (JDK)** installed and the Android **software development kit (SDK)** updated (you need API 22 with the LibGDX version [1.6.4]); otherwise, a simple Google search will do. The steps are OS-free and we will use Windows to implement them.

We will cover the following topics in this chapter:

- Downloading and installing IntelliJ IDEA
- Setting up the LibGDX project and importing it to IntelliJ IDEA
- Running and debugging the game

LibGDX 3D API overview

LibGDX is a Java cross-platform game development framework that released its first version in 2009. It lets you go as low-level as you want to and gives you direct access to all kinds of areas of development. It also comes with an OpenGL ES 2.0 and 3.0 wrapper interface, which is the one that lets us perform 3D development.

3D development with LibGDX already has a nice array of games under its belt already. The following screenshot shows a very popular game called Grandpa's Table, which is available on Android, iOS, and Amazon:

The following is a screenshot of an Android game named Apparatus:

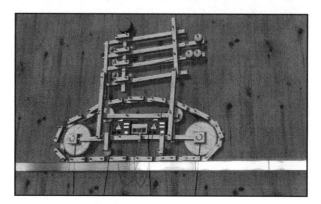

The following screenshot is of the game Ingress, which is available on Android and iOS:

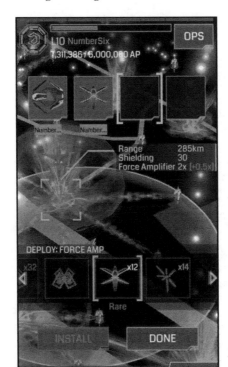

These are just a few of the most popular games out there.

We will not only cover as much as we can from this 3D API—to get the most of it and show a general structure for how to keep things organized and optimal—but also the use of other LibGDX tools to get the most of the framework too.

Downloading IntelliJ IDEA Community Edition

Download the latest version of IntelliJ IDEACommunity Edition for Java developers from `https://www.jetbrains.com/idea/download/`; it will suggest the download versions compatible with your current operating system. Select the version that best suits your operating system platform, which will either be 32-bit or 64-bit.

At the time of writing this book, IntelliJ IDEA Community Edition (14.1.4) is the latest version.

LibGDX project setup

At the time of writing this book, LibGDX was in version 1.6.4 and we will use that version. Download the setup app from `http://libgdx.badlogicgames.com/download.html` and open it:

Set up your project name (ours will be called `Space Gladiators`) and package name (ours is `com.deeep.spaceglad`). Enter the game's main class name (ours is `Core`), set the destination path to your preferred directory, and point out the Android SDK directory location.

We will check the **Desktop**, **Android**, and **iOS** project, but leave out **Html** since we will use the Bullet physics API, which doesn't work on HTML because of the **Google Web Toolkit** (**GWT**) backend (for more information, check out `http://www.badlogicgames.com/wordpress/?p=2308`).

From **Extensions**, we'll select **Bullet** (Bullet physics API), **Tools** (Bitmap Font Generator [Hiero], 3D Particle Editor, and TexturePacker), **Controllers** (Controller Input API), and **Ashley** (Entity System API).

LibGDX comes, as you can see, with a lot of very useful tools that you should use for some time and explore them. We'll cover these selected APIs in some depth over the course of this book.

Click on **Generate** and wait. After it is done, open IntelliJ IDEA and click on **Import Project**. Go to your newly created project and look for a file called `build.gradle`, and IntelliJ will do everything else.

Basic use of IntelliJ IDEA with LibGDX

Running and debugging the app with IntelliJ IDEA is as simple as a click, but sometimes, we need to perform extra configurations on the IDE to avoid exceptions.

Running the Android app

Once IntelliJ is done with all the processes, the default app to run will be Android. To run it, click on the Bug or Play buttons to the right of the navigation bar:

Gradle will build and the **Choose Device** dialog will pop up, from which you'll choose the Android device on which you'll run the app (either an emulator or a physical device), for which you just have to plug in your device.

Running the desktop app

To run the desktop app we have to change the default configuration and add the desktop launcher:

1. Click on **android** and select **Edit Configurations**; the **Run/Debug Configurations** dialog should pop up.
2. Click on the **+** icon at the top left of it and select **Application**.
3. Name it desktop. In the **Main class** field, select DesktopLauncher. For **Working directory**, go to your Android project and double-click the assets folder.
4. Click on the **Use Classpath of module** field, select **desktop**, and then click on the **OK** button at the bottom.

Now instead of **android** at the top, you'll see **desktop**. You can run or debug with the two buttons to the right of it.

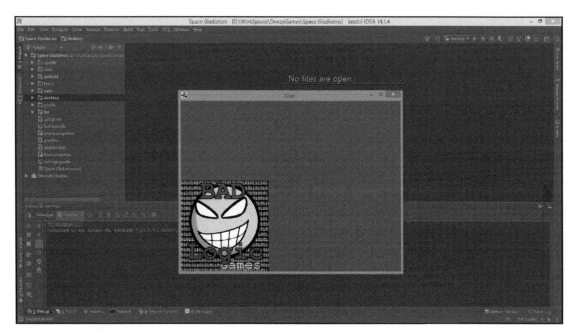

Summary

In this chapter, we introduced IntelliJ IDEA and its basic use; we also explained how to download and install it, and set up LibGDX Project for 3D work. We configured our work environment and launched the Android application into an actual device and the desktop application.

In the next chapter, we'll take the plunge to it and learn about LibGDX's 3D rendering API, perspective camera, 3D workflow, and more.

2
An Extra Dimension

Now that everything is set up, we can move onto the more interesting stuff, (the reason you bought this book), work in three dimensions! This requires new camera techniques: the third dimension adds a new axis instead of having just the x and y grid; a slightly different workflow, and lastly, new render methods are required to draw our game. In this chapter, you'll learn the basics of this workflow to have a sense of what's coming, such as moving, scaling, materials, environment, and some others, and we will move systematically between them, one step at a time.

In this chapter, we will cover the following topics:

- Camera techniques
- Workflow
- LibGDX's 3D rendering API
- Math

Camera techniques

The goal of this book is to successfully create a shooter game, as stated earlier. In order to achieve this, we will start with the basics: making a simple first-person camera. We will facilitate the functions and math that LibGDX contains.

Since you have probably used LibGDX more than once, you will be familiar with the concepts of the camera in 2D. The way 3D works is more or less the same, except there is a z axis now for the depth. However, instead of an `OrthographicCamera` class, a `PerspectiveCamera` class is used to set up the 3D environment. Creating a 3D camera is just as easy as creating a 2D camera. The constructor of a `PerspectiveCamera` class requires three arguments: the field of vision, camera width, and camera height. The camera width and height are known from 2D cameras, the field of vision is new.

The initialization of a `PerspectiveCamera` class looks like this:

```
float FoV = 67;
PerspectiveCamera camera = new PerspectiveCamera(FoV,
Gdx.graphics.getWidth(), Gdx.graphics.getHeight());
```

The first argument, field of vision, describes the angle the first-person camera can see.

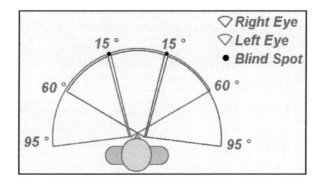

The preceding figure gives a good idea of what the field of view is. Values up to 100 are used for first-person shooters. Values higher than 100 confuse the player and with a lower field of vision, the player is bound to see less.

We will continue where we left off in `Chapter 1`, *Setting Up Your Development Environment*, with an empty project. We will start by doing something exciting, such as drawing a cube on the screen!

Drawing a cube

First things first! Let's create a camera. Earlier, we showed the difference between a 2D and 3D camera, so let's put that to use. Start by creating a new class on your main package (ours is `com.deeep.spaceglad`) and name it however you like.

The following imports are used on our test:

```
import com.badlogic.gdx.ApplicationAdapter;
import com.badlogic.gdx.Gdx;
import com.badlogic.gdx.graphics.Color;
import com.badlogic.gdx.graphics.GL20;
import com.badlogic.gdx.graphics.PerspectiveCamera;
import com.badlogic.gdx.graphics.VertexAttributes;

import com.badlogic.gdx.graphics.g3d.*;
import com.badlogic.gdx.graphics.g3d.attributes.ColorAttribute;
import com.badlogic.gdx.graphics.g3d.environment.DirectionalLight;
import com.badlogic.gdx.graphics.g3d.utils.ModelBuilder;
```

Create a class member called cam of type PerspectiveCamera:

```
public PerspectiveCamera cam;
```

Now, this camera needs to be initialized and configured. This will be done in the create method as shown below:

```
public void create() {
    cam = new PerspectiveCamera(67, Gdx.graphics.getWidth(),
    Gdx.graphics.getHeight());
    cam.position.set(10f, 10f, 10f);
    cam.lookAt(0,0,0);
    cam.near = 1f;
    cam.far = 300f;
    cam.update();
}
```

In the preceding code snippet, we are setting the position of the camera and looking toward a point set at 0, 0, 0. Next up is getting a cube ready to draw. In 2D, it was possible to draw textures but they were flat. In 3D, models are used. Later on, we will import those models. But, for now, we will start with generated models.

LibGDX offers a convenient class to build simple models such as spheres, cubes, cylinders, and many more you can choose from. Let's add two more class members, Model and ModelInstance. The Model class contains all the information on what to draw and the resources that go along with it. The ModelInstance class has information on the whereabouts of the model, such as the location, rotation, and scale of the model.

```
public Model model;
public ModelInstance instance;
```

Add these class members. We will use the overridden `create` function to initialize our new class members.

```
public void create() {
    ...
    ModelBuilder modelBuilder = new ModelBuilder();
    Material mat = new
    Material(ColorAttribute.createDiffuse(Color.BLUE));
    model = modelBuilder.createBox(5, 5, 5, mat,
    VertexAttributes.Usage.Position |
    VertexAttributes.Usage.Normal);
    instance = new ModelInstance(model);
}
```

We use a `ModelBuilder` class to create a box. The box will need a material and a color. A material is an object that holds different attributes. You can add as many as you would want. The attributes passed on to the material change the way models are perceived and shown on the screen. For example, we can add `FloatAttribute.createShininess(8f)` after the `ColorAttribute` class, which will make the box shine with lights around it. There are more complex configurations possible, but we will leave that for now.

With the `ModelBuilder` class, we will create a box of (5, 5, 5). Then we will pass the material in the constructor, and the fifth argument are attributes for the specific box we will create. We use a bitwise operator to combine a position attribute and a normal attribute. We tell the model that it has a position attribute because every cube needs a position, and the normal attribute is to make sure the lighting works and the cube is drawn as we want it to be drawn. These attributes are passed down to openGL on which LibGDX is built.

Now, we are almost ready to draw our first cube but there are two things missing. Firstly, a batch to draw to. When designing 2D games in LibGDX a `SpriteBatch` class is used. However, since we are not using sprites anymore, but rather models, we will use a `ModelBatch` class, which is the equivalent for models. And lastly, we will have to create an environment and add lights to it. For that, we will need two more class members:

```
public ModelBatch modelBatch;
public Environment environment;
```

And they are to be initialized, just like the other class members:

```
public void create() {
    ....
    modelBatch = new ModelBatch();
    environment = new Environment();
    environment.set(new
    ColorAttribute(ColorAttribute.AmbientLight,
    0.4f, 0.4f, 0.4f, 1f));
    environment.add(new DirectionalLight().set(0.8f, 0.8f, 0.8f, -
    1f, -0.8f, -0.2f));
}
```

Here, we add two lights: an ambient light, which lights up everything that is being drawn (a general light source for the environment), and a directional light, which has a direction (most similar to a "sun" type of source). In general, for lights, you can experiment with directions, colors, and different types. Another type of light (`PointLight`) can be compared to a flashlight.

Both lights start with three arguments for the color, which won't make a difference yet as we don't have any textures. The directional light's constructor is followed by a direction. This direction can be seen as a vector.

Now, we are all set to draw our environment and the model in it, as shown in the following code:

```
@Override
public void render() {
    Gdx.gl.glViewport(0, 0, Gdx.graphics.getWidth(),
    Gdx.graphics.getHeight());
    Gdx.gl.glClear(GL20.GL_COLOR_BUFFER_BIT |
    GL20.GL_DEPTH_BUFFER_BIT);

    modelBatch.begin(cam);
    modelBatch.render(instance, environment);
    modelBatch.end();
}
```

It directly renders our cube. The `ModelBatch` class behaves just like `SpriteBatch`, as can be seen if we run it; it has to be started (`begin`), then we ask for it to render and give it parameters (models and `environment` in our case). Then then make it stop.

We should not forget to release any resources that our game allocated. The model we created allocates memory that should be disposed of.

```
@Override
public void dispose() {
    model.dispose();
}
```

Now, we can look at our beautiful cube! However, it's only very static and empty. We will add some movement to it in our next subsection!

Translation

Translating, rotating, and scaling are a bit different from the equivalents in a 2D game. They're slightly more mathematical. The easier part is the vectors. We will now use Vector3D instead of Vector2D, which is essentially the same; it merely adds another dimension.

Let's take a look at some basic operations with 3D models. We will use the cube that we previously created.

With translation we are able to move the model along all three axes.

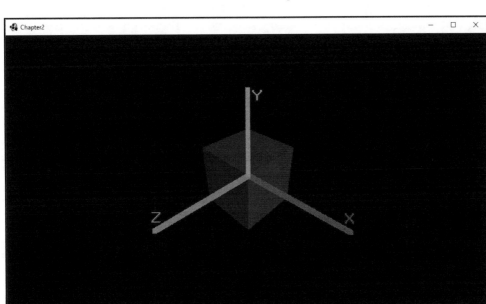

Let's create a function that moves our cube along the *x* axis. We will add a member variable to our class to store the position in for now. A `Vector3` class:

```
Vector3 position = new Vector3();
private void movement() {
    instance.transform.getTranslation(position);
    position.x += Gdx.graphics.getDeltaTime();
    instance.transform.setTranslation(position);
}
```

The preceding code snippet retrieves the translation and adds delta time to the x attribute of the translation. Then we set the translation of `ModelInstance`. The 3D library returns the translation slightly differently. We will pass a vector and it will get adjusted to the current state of the object. We have to call this function every time the game updates. Therefore, we will put it in our `render` loop before we start drawing:

```
@Override
public void render() {
    movement();
    ...
}
```

It might seem like the cube is moving diagonally, but that's because of the angle of our camera. In fact, it's moving toward one face of the cube. That was easy! It's only slightly annoying that it moves out of bounds after a short while. Therefore, we will change the `movement` function to contain some user input handling:

```
private void movement() {
    instance.transform.getTranslation(position);
    if(Gdx.input.isKeyPressed(Input.Keys.W)){
        position.x+=Gdx.graphics.getDeltaTime();
    }
    if(Gdx.input.isKeyPressed(Input.Keys.D)){
        position.z+=Gdx.graphics.getDeltaTime();
    }
    if(Gdx.input.isKeyPressed(Input.Keys.A)){
        position.z-=Gdx.graphics.getDeltaTime();
    }
    if(Gdx.input.isKeyPressed(Input.Keys.S)){
        position.x-=Gdx.graphics.getDeltaTime();
    }
    instance.transform.setTranslation(position);
}
```

The rewritten `movement` function retrieves our position, updates it based on the keys that are pressed, and sets the translation of our model instance.

Rotation

Rotation is slightly different from 2D, since there are multiple axes on which we can rotate, namely, the *x*, *y*, and *z* axes. We will now create a function to showcase the rotation of the model. First, let's create a function in which we can rotate an object on all axes:

```
private void rotate() {
    if (Gdx.input.isKeyPressed(Input.Keys.NUM_1))
        instance.transform.rotate(Vector3.X,
        Gdx.graphics.getDeltaTime() * 100);
    if (Gdx.input.isKeyPressed(Input.Keys.NUM_2))
        instance.transform.rotate(Vector3.Y,
        Gdx.graphics.getDeltaTime() * 100);
    if (Gdx.input.isKeyPressed(Input.Keys.NUM_3))
        instance.transform.rotate(Vector3.Z,
        Gdx.graphics.getDeltaTime() * 100);
}
```

And let's not forget to call this function from the `render` loop, after we call the `movement` function:

```
@Override
public void render() {
    ...
    rotate();
}
```

If we press the number keys *1*, *2*, or *3*, we can rotate our model. The first argument of the `rotate` function is the axis to rotate on. The second argument is the number of rotations. These functions are to add a rotation. We can also set the value of an axis, instead of adding a rotation, with the following function:

```
instance.transform.setToRotation(Vector3.Z,  Gdx.graphics.getDeltaTime() *
100);
```

Let's say, we want to set all three axis rotations at the same time; we can't simply call the `setToRotation` function three times in a row for each axis, as they eliminate any other rotation done before that. Luckily, LibGDX has a function that is able to take all three axes:

```
float rotation;
private void rotate() {
    rotation = (rotation + Gdx.graphics.getDeltaTime() * 100) %
    360;
    instance.transform.setFromEulerAngles(0, 0, rotation);
}
```

The previous function will continuously rotate our cube; however, we face one last problem. We can't seem to move the cube! The `setFromEulerAngles` function clears all the translation and rotation properties. Lucky for us `setFromEulerAngles` returns a `Matrix4` type, so we can chain and call another function from it, for example, a function that translates the matrix. For this, we use the `trn(x, y, z)` function (short for translate). Now we can update our `rotation` function, although it also translates:

```
instance.transform.setFromEulerAngles(0, 0,  rotation).trn(position.x,
position.y, position.z);
```

Now, we can set our cube to a rotation, and translate it! These are the most basic operations and we will use them a lot throughout the book. As you can see, this function does both the rotation and translation. So, we can remove the last line in our `movement` function:

```
instance.transform.setTranslation(position);
```

Our latest `rotate` function looks like this:

```
private void rotate() {
    rotation = (rotation + Gdx.graphics.getDeltaTime() * 100) %
    360;
    instance.transform.setFromEulerAngles(0, 0,
    rotation).trn(position.x, position.y, position.z);
}
```

The `setFromEulerAngles` function will be extracted to a function of its own, as it serves multiple purposes now and is not solely bound to our `rotate` function:

```
private void updateTransformation(){
    instance.transform.setFromEulerAngles(0, 0,
    rotation).trn(position.x, position.y,
    position.z).scale(scale,scale,scale);
}
```

This function should be called after we've calculated our rotation and translation:

```
public void render() {
    rotate();
    movement();
    updateTransformation();
    ...
}
```

Scaling

We've almost performed all of the transformations we can apply to models. The last one described in this book is the scaling a model. LibGDX luckily contains all the required functions and methods for this. Let's extend our previous example and make our box grow and shrink over time.

We will first create a function that increments and subtracts from a `scale` variable:

```
boolean increment;
float scale = 1;
void scale(){
        if(increment) {
            scale = (scale + Gdx.graphics.getDeltaTime()/5);
            if (scale >= 1.5f)  {
                increment = false;
            } else {
                scale = (scale - Gdx.graphics.getDeltaTime()/5);
```

```
                        if(scale <= 0.5f)
                            increment = true;
                }
        }
```

To apply this scaling, we can adjust our `updateTransformation` function to include it:

```
        private void updateTransformation(){
            instance.transform.setFromEulerAngles(0, 0,
            rotation).trn(position.x, position.y,
            position.z).scale(scale,scale,scale);
        }
```

Our `render` method should now include the scaling function as well:

```
        public void render() {
            rotate();
            movement();
            scale();
            updateTransformation();
            ...
        }
```

And there you go, we can now successfully move, rotate, and scale our cube!

Summary

In this chapter, you learned about the workflow of the LibGDX 3D API. We will now be able to apply multiple kinds of transformation to a model, and understand the difference between 2D and 3D. You also learned how to apply materials to models to change its appearance and create cool effects.

Note that there's plenty more information that you can learn about 3D and a lot of practice to go with it to fully understand it. There are also subjects we haven't covered here, such as how to create your own materials, and how to make and use shaders. There's plenty of scope for learning and experimenting.

In the next chapter, we will start to apply the theory that you learned in this chapter and work toward an actual game! We will also go into the environment and lights as well as collision detection in more detail. So, there's plenty to look forward to.

3
Working toward a Prototype

In this chapter, we will explain and develop a prototype of our game using only basic methods of the 3D API, basic Bullet Physics API, and Scene2D for the UI. It's important to cover a prototype development to see quick results and focus on the main mechanics of the game, this is also important for game design and fast iterations, hence being able to improve gameplay before it's too late.

Note that starting from here, you can see the source code in our repository (`https://githu b.com/DeeepGames/SpaceGladiators`) and get images and other files from the `assets` folder of it in the `Android` project folder. Make sure to be in the **Branch: Prototype** to see the code used in this chapter. Branches in GitHub are seen on the middle-left side of the link.

In this chapter, we will cover the following topics:

- Creating our world
- Moving the camera and our player
- Understanding Bullet Physics
- Adding enemies and a chase mechanic
- Understanding Scene2D (UI)
- Using screens

Creating our world

We will build our world and talk about what's going on inside our structure. First, we'll start implementing our game world, the UI, and other screens later.

Creating our structure

First, we will set up a structure to work with and keep things organized. We will make a small image that shows how the structure is made:

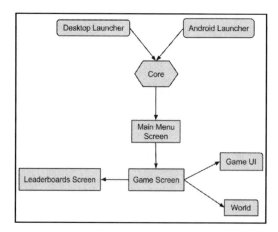

The `DesktopLauncher.java` and `AndroidLauncher.java` contain the **Core** that will run our screens. The Core will call the first screen, the **Main Menu Screen**; from there we can go to the **Game Screen** or **Leaderboards Screen**, and move between them.

As good practice and to keep our motivation up, we will first build a Game Screen and an actual game to check design failures and see fast gameplay.

First, we'll configure `DesktopLauncher.java` using the following code:

```
public class DesktopLauncher {
    public static void main(String[] arg) {
        LwjglApplicationConfiguration config = new
        LwjglApplicationConfiguration();
        config.width = (int) Core.VIRTUAL_WIDTH;
        config.height = (int) Core.VIRTUAL_HEIGHT;
        new LwjglApplication(new Core(), config);
    }
}
```

We will add a couple of variables to the configuration, and cast them to integers that we'll add into the `Core.java` class. This is to keep a screen ratio.

Let's fire up `Core.java` and write this:

```java
public class Core extends ApplicationAdapter {
    public static final float VIRTUAL_WIDTH = 960;
    public static final float VIRTUAL_HEIGHT = 540;
    Screen screen;
    @Override
    public void create() {
        Gdx.input.setCatchBackKey(true);
        setScreen(new GameScreen(this));
    }
    @Override
    public void render() {
        Gdx.gl.glClearColor(0, 0, 0, 1);
        Gdx.gl.glClear(GL20.GL_COLOR_BUFFER_BIT |
        GL20.GL_DEPTH_BUFFER_BIT);
        screen.render(Gdx.graphics.getDeltaTime());
    }
    @Override
    public void resize(int width, int height) {
        screen.resize(width, height);
    }
    public void setScreen(Screen screen) {
        if (this.screen != null) {
            this.screen.hide();
            this.screen.dispose();
        }
        this.screen = screen;
        if (this.screen != null) {
            this.screen.show();
            this.screen.resize(Gdx.graphics.getWidth(),
            Gdx.graphics.getHeight());
        }
    }
}
```

First, we will set up a VIRTUAL_WIDTH and VIRTUAL_HEIGHT, so as to have a standard screen ratio. We will choose 960×540 as the ratio so it can fit most Android devices' screens and add code for this stretch to be automatic.

On `create()`, we'll catch the software-back button from Android devices, so the app will not close when it's pressed. Once we set the screen, create a new GameScreen, and send the app itself to it (the `this` keyword); we'll create this class in a minute.

On render(), we will need calls to clear the screen, set the clear color to black (0, 0, 0, 1), and the method necessary for 3D (GL20.GL_COLOR_BUFFER_BIT | GL20.GL_DEPTH_BUFFER_BIT). Then, we'll draw our screen and send it the time that passed for every frame (Gdx.graphics.getDeltaTime()).

Resize will only contain our screen and its resize method call, which will need the new width and height.

And lastly, we'll create a new method called setScreen(...). It will receive the new screen, take the necessary steps to set it up, and dispose the screen that was already running, if there was any.

Game screen

Game screen will contain everything our game needs to draw its game world and UI. Let's create a new class called GameScreen.java and put it on a new package called screens:

```java
public class GameScreen implements Screen {
    Core game;
    GameWorld gameWorld;
    public GameScreen(Core game) {
        this.game = game;
        gameWorld = new GameWorld();
        Gdx.input.setCursorCatched(true);
    }
    @Override
    public void render(float delta) {
        gameWorld.render(delta);
    }
    @Override
    public void resize(int width, int height) {
        gameWorld.resize(width, height);
    }
    @Override
    public void dispose() {
        gameWorld.dispose();
    }
    // empty methods from Screen
}
```

Set it to implement `Screen`, and you will be asked to implement methods from it; we'll do that next:

- `GameScreen()`: This constructor will save an instance of our app for later use. It will create a new `GameWorld()` and catch the cursor (from our PC), so we don't see it while playing.
- `Render()`: This will draw the world and receive the delta time.
- `Resize(...)`: This is called from the `Core` class, receiving `width` and `height`, and we'll set the game world to resize itself.
- `Dispose()`: This will make all necessary disposes for when the app is closed. They are mainly native objects (OpenGL).

All other methods need to be implemented, but we will not use them.

A simple playground

Now, we have prepared a screen for our game to draw on. However, our game is still a bit empty. So, let's create a floor and four simple walls to contain our game (so the player won't fall off the ground), and a camera. We will use techniques shown in `Chapter 2`, *An Extra Dimension* for this. First, we will create a `GameWorld` class. `GameWorld` is the class holding all the data inside our world. It handles all the elements inside the world, such as obstacles, enemies, collisions, AI, and so on. This is a big step in getting our prototype and is one of the places where development goes fast as we don't have to worry about getting everything perfect.

Game world

The `GameWorld` class has a constructor and three main functions that are the same as `GameScreen`.

Our constructor is called by `GameScreen` and will, for now, not take any arguments. In here, we will initialize all the objects we'll use. We will need a `PerspectiveCamera` class, an `Environment` class, and a `ModelBatch` class to start off with.

The camera is used to view our models and possibly sprites; the `Environment` handles lighting; and the `ModelBatch` is used to render models. If you were to use sprites in the game, you can also use a `SpriteBatch` class.

Let's create a new class called GameWorld.java and place it in the default package. The initialization will look like this:

```
public class GameWorld {
    private static final float FOV = 67F;
    private ModelBatch batch;
    private Environment environment;
    private PerspectiveCamera cam;
public GameWorld() {
    initPersCamera();
    initEnvironment();
    initModelBatch();
}
private void initPersCamera() {
    perspectiveCamera = new PerspectiveCamera(FOV,
    Core.VIRTUAL_WIDTH, Core.VIRTUAL_HEIGHT);
    perspectiveCamera.position.set(30f, 40f, 30f);
    perspectiveCamera.lookAt(0f, 0f, 0f);
    perspectiveCamera.near = 1f;
    perspectiveCamera.far = 300f;
    perspectiveCamera.update();
}
private void initEnvironment() {
    environment = new Environment();
    environment.set(new ColorAttribute(ColorAttribute.AmbientLight,
    0.3f, 0.3f, 0.3f, 1f));
}
private void initModelBatch() {
    modelBatch = new ModelBatch();
}

/*The ModelBatch is one of the objects, which require disposing, hence we
add it to the dispose function. */
public void dispose() {
    modelBatch.dispose();
}
/*With the camera set we can now fill in the resize function as well*/
public void resize(int width, int height) {
    perspectiveCamera .viewportHeight = height;
    perspectiveCamera .viewportWidth = width;
}
//and set up the render function with the modelbatch
public void render(float delta) {
    modelBatch.begin(perspectiveCamera);
    modelBatch.end();
}
```

Note that the `render` function takes our `delta` time as a parameter as it also handles updates to our entities.

Now, you should be able to launch the game without errors. You won't see anything yet as we still have to add things in our world.

Adding visuals

Now, let's create the room. We drew some boxes in `Chapter 2`, *An Extra Dimensions*; however, this time around, we will change it a little bit. We will make use of an entity system called **Ashley**, which comes with LibGDX.

Introduction to Ashley

Ashley is an **Entity Management System** included in LibGDX and the one we will work with in this book. We've chosen to use Ashley because it is one of the best at teaching good practices when dealing with a lot of similar dynamic objects with a few differences in their properties. An example could be an enemy versus an obstacle. They both have a position, a model, and a rotation; however, only one of them can move and attack the player. We can manage the differences in properties using the Ashley components and system. Components will be added to entities to differentiate them, and systems put these differences into effect in our game; separate systems will be created to manage a specific family of entities (players, monsters, and so on) based on the components we choose to add. We will start with components as it is essential for us to continue making systems, and then progress with creating our entities. Once the components are finished, we can start creating systems for our entity families and we can see the bigger picture much more clearly.

Components

Components are a great way to assign properties to entities. They allow you to specify the attributes that apply to specific entities. An enemy might have a position component, a model component, a velocity component, and a render component, while an obstacle might have just the position component, the model component, and the render component. After this brief introduction, we will get started with a simple component.

Model component

Now, we will conisder what kind of components we will need. We can do that by looking at overlapping areas of information. A good example is 3D models. Every instance drawn on the screen will have some kind of model; whether that is a character, a wall, or a bullet, they all have a model in common. Therefore, we will create `ModelComponent.java` and place it in a package named `components`.

When we look back at `Chapter 2`, *An Extra Dimension*, we see how we instantiated a simple model and drew it on the screen. In order to draw a model on the screen, we need a reference to the model itself and a position to draw it on. We also need `ModelInstance` for transformations on the model, as shown in the following code:

```java
public class ModelComponent extends Component {
    public Model model;
    public ModelInstance instance;

    public ModelComponent(Model model, float x, float y, float z) {
        this.model = model;
        this.instance = new ModelInstance(model, new
        Matrix4().setToTranslation(x, y, z));
    }
}
```

There it is! This is a small data container for objects. Now, let's get this to work with our game. Ashley makes use of the `Entity` class. An `Entity` object contains multiple components, and is stored within an `Engine` class. So, let's give our `GameWorld` an Ashley engine.

Let's create a local field with the type `Engine` and call it `engine`. This is located in the `com.badlogic.ashley.core.Engine;` package. Now, we can construct it with the default constructor. We can do this in the constructor of `GameWorld`. The following code snippet (`engine = new Engine();`) shows the creation of an `Entity` object, adding of a component, and adding that entity with the component to the system.

First, we will create a model:

```java
ModelBuilder modelBuilder = new ModelBuilder();
Material boxMaterial = new
Material(ColorAttribute.createDiffuse(Color.WHITE),
ColorAttribute.createSpecular(Color.RED),
FloatAttribute.createShininess(16f));
Model box = modelBuilder.createBox(5, 5, 5, boxMaterial,
VertexAttributes.Usage.Position | VertexAttributes.Usage.Normal);
```

Then, we will create the entity:

```
Entity entity = new Entity();
entity.add(new ModelComponent(box,10,10,10));
engine.addEntity(entity);
```

The creation of the model should look familiar from `Chapter 2`, *An Extra Dimension*. The entity now exists in the system. However, nothing is done with it. This is where the `EntitySystem` class comes in to place.

Systems and Ashley's engine

Components don't do anything on their own; they need to be put to use somehow. That is the role of the systems. The systems classes are created by extending the `EntitySystem` class from the Ashley library. Each of our systems must have an `update()` function and an `addedToEngine()` function. Everything else is up to you. The `update()` method gets called every game tick, and the `addedToEngine()` is called once the system is added to the engine. We don't directly call this method anywhere in our code; it gets called by Ashley's `Engine` class. Now, we will want to draw our box on the screen; for this, we will create a new class called `RenderSystem`.

Render system

The render system will need to iterate over all the entities containing `ModelComponent` and draw these to the screen. This sounds easy, right? Well, it is! It can be seen here:

```
public class RenderSystem extends EntitySystem {
    private ImmutableArray<Entity> entities;
    private ModelBatch batch;
    private Environment environment;
    public RenderSystem(ModelBatch batch, Environment environment) {
        this.batch = batch;
        this.environment = environment;
    }
    public void addedToEngine(Engine e) {
        entities =
        e.getEntitiesFor(Family.all(ModelComponent.class).get());
    }
    public void update(float delta) {
        for (int i = 0; i < entities.size(); i++) {
            ModelComponent mod =
            entities.get(i).getComponent(ModelComponent.class);
            batch.render(mod.instance, environment);
```

```
                }
            }
        }
```

The `ImmutableArray` is an array list reference from the entity system. This array will contain references to all the entities that we filter for. In the `addedToEngine` function, it's shown how this is done. We want to get a list of all the entities containing `ModelComponent`. We filter using a `Family` class. There are three family functions: `Family.all(...)`, `Family.one(...)`, and `Family.exclude(...)`. When `Family.all(...)` is used, `ImmutableArray` will only contain entities that have all the components given, that is:

```
entities =
e.getEntitiesFor(Family.all(comp1.class,comp2.class,comp3.class).get());
```

The `ImmutableArray` will return with all the entities containing the following components: `comp1`, `comp2`, and `comp3`, along with other possible components. When `Family.one(...)` is used, the entity will only require one of those components to be listed. Additionally, when `Family.exclude(...)` is used, then none of the entities in the bag will contain any of the components given.

Now, the last thing we have to do is to add the system to the world. This can be done with the following function:

```
engine.addSystem(new RenderSystem(modelBatch, environment));
```

When all is put in place, for now in the constructor will do, we can see a nice cube.

Adding physics and collisions

So, now we have the ability to create entities. However, these entities will have to interact once they collide. For example, when an enemy hits the player, damage should be done. Or when the player hits the floor, it should not fall through.

Essentially, this can be done the same way as it is done with 2D, except for the fact that one more axis requires to be checked. First we will look at simple collision methods, where we will encapsulate the object to be checked in the smallest rectangle possible.

One way to do it is where two rectangles are checked for collision. The condition for the collision would be when all the axes of one rectangle are contained in the other rectangle. However, this adds a lot of performance loss as every object will have to be checked. Now, special techniques could be used to achieve a higher performance boost, but instead of coming up with this ourselves and taking the time to write this piece of code, we will use a library.

Bullet Physics and Bullet system

Bullet Physics is an ideal way of handling all the collisions and has a lot of extra functionality we could make use of, such as gravity. It's a library written in C++. Although all the basic functionality can be accessed via the **Java Native Interface (JNI)**, the library also contains some extra helping functions, which we will use.

Collision detection is often processed in two phases, a broad phase and a narrow phase. The broad phase calculates possible collisions between objects, and the narrow phase makes sure whether the objects collided. Here's an example.

The following 2D map is split up in nine cells. Every cell contains objects. The computer can quickly see the fact that objects from cell A1 can't collide with objects from cell C3. It can, however, add all the objects from cell A1 in an array that will be passed to the narrow phase. The narrow phase could be pixel perfect collision detection here. It will check all the objects from the list that the broad phase passed, and this makes sure whether a collision indeed did happen or not.

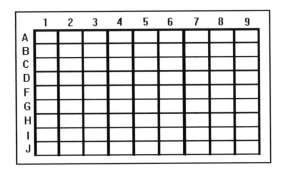

One technique Bullet uses for the broad phase is the **Axis-Aligned Bounding Box (AABB)**. This is a performant way of collision detection. AABB sorts all the bounding boxes on one axis and sees which boxes overlap. This is really nifty and is easy to use. We will be use this in our prototype.

For collision checking with Bullet, it will need to have a reference to all the objects that will be used. These references are stored in a so called btCollisionWorld class. This class contains links to the Bullet.dll via JNI and has access to a variety of functions. These functions allow us to add new objects to the world, describe the way collision detection should be handled, and gives us an opportunity to add callbacks for whenever a collision happens. Another class that extends to btCollisionWorld is btDynamicsWorld. This class, as the name suggests, is to add dynamic entities, for example, with gravity. This is useful as the player will have gravity and will be able to move. Thus, we can say that the player is a dynamic object.

Before we get ahead of ourselves, we will add a new class. This class will hold the position and angle of any static or dynamic physics object and will extend the btMotionState class from the Bullet library:

```
public class MotionState extends btMotionState {
    private final Matrix4 transform;

    public MotionState(final Matrix4 transform) {
        this.transform = transform;
    }
    @Override
    public void getWorldTransform(final Matrix4 worldTrans) {
        worldTrans.set(transform);
    }
    @Override
    public void setWorldTransform(final Matrix4 worldTrans) {
        transform.set(worldTrans);
    }
}
```

Now, we will start implementing the collision-related components. First up is BulletComponent. This component will contain all data that is required to function within a bullet environment:

```
public class BulletComponent extends Component{
    public MotionState motionState;
    public btRigidBody.btRigidBodyConstructionInfo bodyInfo;
    public btCollisionObject body;
}
```

It contains a motionState object for information about the position and angle of the physical object.

Citing straight from the Bullet API, btRigidBodyConstructionInfo provides information to create a rigid body. Setting the mass to zero creates a fixed (non-dynamic), rigid body. For dynamic objects, you can use the collision shape to approximate the local inertia tensor; otherwise, use the zero vector (default argument). You can use the motion state to synchronize the world transform between physics and graphics objects. Also, if the motion state is provided, the rigid body will initialize its initial world transform from the motion state.

The btCollisionObject is the object that can eventually be added to our bullet environment and is used to manage collision detection objects.

To show how it's put to use, we will create a function that accepts a model and a position, and returns an Ashley entity. Let's create a class called EntityFactory.java, place it on a package called managers, and add:

```java
public static Entity createStaticEntity(Model model, float x, float y,
float z) {
    final BoundingBox boundingBox = new BoundingBox();
    model.calculateBoundingBox(boundingBox);
    Vector3 tmpV = new Vector3();
    btCollisionShape col = new
    btBoxShape(tmpV.set(boundingBox.getWidth() * 0.5f,
    boundingBox.getHeight() * 0.5f, boundingBox.getDepth() * 0.5f));
    Entity entity = new Entity();
    ModelComponent modelComponent = new ModelComponent(model, x, y,
    z);
    entity.add(modelComponent);
    BulletComponent bulletComponent = new BulletComponent();
    bulletComponent.bodyInfo = new
    btRigidBody.btRigidBodyConstructionInfo(0, null, col,
    Vector3.Zero);
    bulletComponent.body = new
    btRigidBody(bulletComponent.bodyInfo);
    bulletComponent.body.userData = entity;
    bulletComponent.motionState = new
    MotionState(modelComponent.instance.transform);
    ((btRigidBody)
    bulletComponent.body).setMotionState
    (bulletComponent.motionState);
    entity.add(bulletComponent);
    return entity;
}
```

First, we will calculate the bounding box that is used for a collision shape, which in turn is required for `btRigidBodyConstructionInfo`. This bounding box is calculated based on the model that's given. For now, we will check for the smallest possible box around a model. This is not very accurate, but it saves a lot of performance and eases the creation of the prototype.

We will then create our Ashely `entity`. First, we will add `ModelComponent` so that we can see our physics object in the world. Once that's done, we will add `BulletComponent` and initialize each of the fields:

```
btRigidBody.btRigidBodyConstructionInfo(0, null, col, Vector3.Zero);
```

With this constructor, we will assign no mass to the object; hence the , no initial motion state, the collision shape we just calculated, and no starting inertia. This creates a static rigid body.

The `createStaticEntity` function is used in the following way:

```
engine.addEntity(createStaticEntity(model, 0, 0, 0));
```

When we add a new `createStaticEntity` generated entity to our system, nothing special will happen. That is partly because it's a static physics object, but also because we have no physics system in place yet.

The Bullet system is where all the physics is set up. To use the collision in cooperation with the entity system we have, we will create a new system: the Bullet system. This system will handle all the detections and collisions of it. As always, we will start with an empty class, extending the `EntitySystem` class. As mentioned earlier, bullet needs references to the objects in order to check them. So, it's vital for us to register any object that requires collision checking. This can be done with the `EntityListener` interface.

We override the `addedToEngine` function so we can set a filter for just collision components with the `EntityListener` interface and register it.

Bullet has its own collision world. In this world, it will apply forces, such as gravity and collision forces, and calculate collisions. The entities we made earlier have the capability to work along with bullet's own collision world. Lastly, we will set the gravity of the entity world.

Bullet has different kinds of collision worlds; this can be read at the API of the `Bullet` library. We will work with `btDiscreteDynamicsWorld`. The other worlds are either too complex to talk about in this book or are meant for testing and validation purposes.

First, we will initialize our world. We will start with setting up the `Bullet` library and creating a `defaultCollisionConfiguration` interface. Then, we will create our dispatcher; this gives us support for the collision detection. The `btAxisSweep3` interface is an efficient implementation of the 3D axis sweeps and prune broad phase, and it tells the collision system where to look for collisions (between $-1000, -1000, -1000$ and $1000, 1000, 1000$). With all this information, we can create our collision world. Now, we will create an object that keeps a track of collisions and overlappings, and add that to our collision interface.

As we just discussed, `BulletSystem` will be notified whenever an entity with `BulletComponent` gets added to our entity world. All that's left to do is to add this to our collision world.

This can be seen in our `entityAdded` function.

Now, we will update our collision world and run simulations on it. This is done with `stepSimulation`. We will pass the `deltaTime` as an argument:

```
public void update(float deltaTime) {
    collisionWorld.stepSimulation(deltaTime);
}
/*The only thing that we will have to do is add these entities to the
bullet collision world.*/
public class BulletSystem extends EntitySystem implements EntityListener {
    public final btCollisionConfiguration collisionConfiguration;
    public final btCollisionDispatcher dispatcher;
    public final btBroadphaseInterface broadphase;
    public final btConstraintSolver solver;
    public final btDiscreteDynamicsWorld collisionWorld;
    private btGhostPairCallback ghostPairCallback;
    public int maxSubSteps = 5;
    public float fixedTimeStep = 1f / 60f;
    @Override
    public void addedToEngine(Engine engine) {
        engine.addEntityListener(Family.all(BulletComponent.class).get(),
this);
    }
    public BulletSystem() {
        collisionConfiguration = new
        btDefaultCollisionConfiguration();
        dispatcher = new
        btCollisionDispatcher(collisionConfiguration);
        broadphase = new btAxisSweep3(new Vector3(-1000, -1000,
        -1000), new Vector3(1000, 1000, 1000));
        solver = new btSequentialImpulseConstraintSolver();
        collisionWorld = new btDiscreteDynamicsWorld(dispatcher,
```

```java
        broadphase, solver, collisionConfiguration);
    ghostPairCallback = new btGhostPairCallback();
    broadphase.getOverlappingPairCache().
    setInternalGhostPairCallback(ghostPairCallback);
    this.collisionWorld.setGravity(new Vector3(0, -0.5f, 0));
}
@Override
public void update(float deltaTime) {
    collisionWorld.stepSimulation(deltaTime, maxSubSteps,
    fixedTimeStep);
}
public void dispose() {
    collisionWorld.dispose();
    if (solver != null) solver.dispose();
    if (broadphase != null) broadphase.dispose();
    if (dispatcher != null) dispatcher.dispose();
    if (collisionConfiguration != null)
        collisionConfiguration.dispose();
        ghostPairCallback.dispose();
}
@Override
public void entityAdded(Entity entity) {
    BulletComponent bulletComponent =
    entity.getComponent(BulletComponent.class);
    if (bulletComponent.body != null) {
        collisionWorld.addRigidBody((btRigidBody)
        bulletComponent.body);
    }
}
public void removeBody(Entity entity) {
    BulletComponent comp =
    entity.getComponent(BulletComponent.class);
    if (comp != null)
    collisionWorld.removeCollisionObject(comp.body);
    CharacterComponent character =
    entity.getComponent(CharacterComponent.class);
    if (character != null) {
        collisionWorld.removeAction
        (character.characterController);
        collisionWorld.removeCollisionObject
        (character.ghostObject);
    }
}
@Override
public void entityRemoved(Entity entity) {
}
}
```

Creating a scene

Now that we have created our base with all the systems set to render and manage physics, we can create our scene. For our needs, we can use a simple ground and walls, so, fire up GameWorld and add:

```
public class GameWorld {
    ...
    private Engine engine;
    public BulletSystem bulletSystem;
    public ModelBuilder modelBuilder = new ModelBuilder();

    Model wallHorizontal = modelBuilder.createBox(40, 20, 1,
            new Material(ColorAttribute.createDiffuse(Color.WHITE),
            ColorAttribute.createSpecular(Color.RED), FloatAttribute
            .createShininess(16f)), VertexAttributes.Usage.Position
            | VertexAttributes.Usage.Normal);
            Model wallVertical = modelBuilder.createBox(1, 20, 40,
            new Material(ColorAttribute.createDiffuse(Color.GREEN),
            ColorAttribute.createSpecular(Color.WHITE),
            FloatAttribute.createShininess(16f)),
            VertexAttributes.Usage.Position |
            VertexAttributes.Usage.Normal);
            Model groundModel = modelBuilder.createBox(40, 1, 40,
            new Material(ColorAttribute.createDiffuse(Color.YELLOW),
            ColorAttribute.createSpecular(Color.BLUE),
            FloatAttribute.createShininess(16f)),
            VertexAttributes.Usage.Position
            | VertexAttributes.Usage.Normal);

    public GameWorld(GameUI gameUI) {
        Bullet.init();
        initEnvironment();
        initModelBatch();
        initPersCamera();
        addSystems(gameUI);
        addEntities();
    }

    private void addEntities() {
        createGround();
    }

    private void createGround() {
        engine.addEntity(EntityFactory.createStaticEntity
        (groundModel,0, 0, 0));
        engine.addEntity(EntityFactory.createStaticEntity
```

```
        (wallHorizontal, 0, 10, -20));
    engine.addEntity(EntityFactory.createStaticEntity
        (wallHorizontal, 0, 10, 20));
    engine.addEntity(EntityFactory.createStaticEntity
        (wallVertical, 20, 10, 0));
    engine.addEntity(EntityFactory.createStaticEntity
        (wallVertical, -20, 10, 0));
}

private void addSystems() {
    engine = new Engine();
    engine.addSystem(new RenderSystem(modelBatch, environment));
    engine.addSystem(bulletSystem = new BulletSystem());
}

public void render(float delta) {
    renderWorld(delta);
}

protected void renderWorld(float delta) {
    modelBatch.begin(perspectiveCamera);
    engine.update(delta);
    modelBatch.end();
}

public void dispose() {
    bulletSystem.dispose();
    bulletSystem = null;
    wallHorizontal.dispose();
    wallVertical.dispose();
    groundModel.dispose();
    modelBatch.dispose();
    modelBatch = null;
}
...
}
```

As you can see, there's quite a bunch of stuff added. We got to add `Engine`, `BulletSystem`, `ModelBuilder`, and the ground and wall models as global fields on the class.

On the constructor, we added the call to the `Bullet.init`, method as necessary and mentioned earlier. We added a few more methods to call and added the new systems (render and bullet), and then actually added the ground and walls as entities to the engine with the previous method created, `createStaticEntity`.

The `render` method got a slight cleanup for the next calls. And finally, the dispose `method` got a bunch more of things to call.

When you run it, you should see something like this:

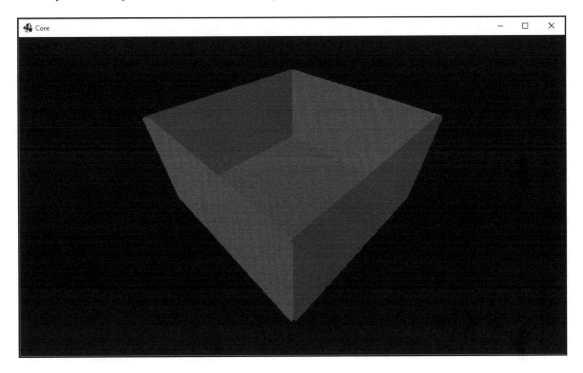

Moving on, let's add some life to it.

Movable characters

There are a few ways to implement moving characters. One of them is to constantly check whether the area in front of the object is clear to move. Another one would be to move, and afterwards check whether the object hits a wall, and reverts to the previous position if that's the case. Bullet has its own character controller that handles all collisions and movement.

This character controller will be embedded in `CharacterComponent` along with a few other fields: a ghost object, a ghost shape, a character controller, and two vectors; one for the walking direction and one for the direction the character is facing.

The complete component can be seen as follows:

```
public class CharacterComponent extends Component {
    public btConvexShape ghostShape;
    public btPairCachingGhostObject ghostObject;
    public btKinematicCharacterController characterController;

    public Vector3 characterDirection = new Vector3();
    public Vector3 walkDirection = new Vector3();
}
```

First up is the `ghostShape` component. This is the shape of the character and collisions will be calculated around this shape. The `ghostObject` component is used to keep track of all the collisions and adds a possibility to filter out different collision classes; we will discuss more about this later. And lastly, the `characterController` object requires references to the `ghostObject` component and the `ghostShape` component and calculates movements. Next up is the creation of character entity.

Character entity seems more complex at first sight but is very straightforward. At first, we will create `modelComponent` and apply a standard model to it. Then, we will instantiate the `ghostObject` component and align it to the position of the model. The shape is self-explanatory. We will use a capsule, as our model is also a capsule. We will then let our `ghostObject` component know what shape we will use. The `collisionFlags` object is used for collision filtering. The `characterController` is where it all happens and makes use of our shape and object. We set the `userData` to our entity so that we have access to it at collision checking. We then tell `BulletWorld` that we have a special kind of object, which takes external forces. We also say that it is a character and should respond to any object in our collision world. Add the following lines to `EntityFactory.java`:

```
static {
    modelBuilder = new ModelBuilder();
    playerTexture = new
    Texture(Gdx.files.internal("data/badlogic.jpg"));
    Material material = new
    Material(TextureAttribute.createDiffuse(playerTexture),
    ColorAttribute.createSpecular(1, 1, 1, 1),
    FloatAttribute.createShininess(8f));
    playerModel = modelBuilder.createCapsule(2f, 6f, 16, material,
    VertexAttributes.Usage.Position | VertexAttributes.Usage.Normal
    | VertexAttributes.Usage.TextureCoordinates);
}

private static Entity createCharacter(BulletSystem bulletSystem, float x,
float y, float z) {
    Entity entity = new Entity();
```

```
ModelComponent modelComponent = new ModelComponent(playerModel,
x, y, z);
entity.add(modelComponent);
CharacterComponent characterComponent = new
CharacterComponent();
characterComponent.ghostObject = new btPairCachingGhostObject();
characterComponent.ghostObject.setWorldTransform
(modelComponent.instance.transform);
characterComponent.ghostShape = new btCapsuleShape(2f, 2f);
characterComponent.ghostObject.setCollisionShape
(characterComponent.ghostShape);
characterComponent.ghostObject.setCollisionFlags
(btCollisionObject.CollisionFlags.CF_CHARACTER_OBJECT);
characterComponent.characterController = new
btKinematicCharacterController(characterComponent.ghostObject,
characterComponent.ghostShape, .35f);
characterComponent.ghostObject.userData = entity;
entity.add(characterComponent);
bulletSystem.collisionWorld.addCollisionObject
(entity.getComponent(CharacterComponent.class).ghostObject,
(short)
btBroadphaseProxy.CollisionFilterGroups.CharacterFilter,
(short)
(btBroadphaseProxy.CollisionFilterGroups.AllFilter));
bulletSystem.collisionWorld.addAction(entity.getComponent
(CharacterComponent.class).characterController);
return entity;
}
```

Player component

The player component is specifically tailored toward the player object. It has additional properties that only apply to the player's character, such as health and score, and if you want to go a bit further in game designing, you can add energy and oxygen. We will store these properties a float and reset them to their default value (0 for score and 100 for the remaining) once a new player entity is created in the world. Player resources such as oxygen go from 0 to 100:

```
public class PlayerComponent extends Component {
    public float energy;
    public float oxygen;
    public float health;
    public static int score;
    public PlayerComponent() {
        energy = 100;
```

```
        oxygen = 100;
        health = 100;
        score = 0;
    }
}
```

However, besides these properties, a player also has to be controlled; therefore, it is also in need of `CharacterComponent`. Add to `EntityFactory.java`:

```
public static Entity createPlayer(BulletSystem bulletSystem, float x, float
y, float z) {
    Entity entity = createCharacter(bulletSystem, x, y, z);
    entity.add(new PlayerComponent());
    return entity;
}
```

This will add the properties and the character component so that the player can be moved. However, the character component has to be updated with key inputs from the user. Additionally, a camera will have to be aligned to the character component to make it an actual first-person shooter. This, and more, is done in the player system.

Player system

We will focus on the character component manipulation for now.

There will always only be one player as it is a single player game. The player system requires a reference to this player in order to manipulate the correct character component. This is done by making the system listen for all entities containing `PlayerComponent`. As soon as an entity containing `PlayerComponent` gets added, the references of the `PlayerSystem` will be set. This can be seen in the `entityAdded` function.

If the player reference has been set, the `updateMovement` method will be called upon the execution of the `update` method. In the `updateMovement`, the position and rotation of the camera will be set to that of the player, for example:

```
public class PlayerSystem extends EntitySystem implements EntityListener {
    private Entity player;
    private PlayerComponent playerComponent;
    private CharacterComponent characterComponent;
    private ModelComponent modelComponent;
    private final Vector3 tmp = new Vector3();
    private final Camera camera;
    public PlayerSystem(Camera camera) {
        this.camera = camera;
        this.gameWorld = gameWorld;
```

```
        }

        @Override
        public void addedToEngine(Engine engine) {
            engine.addEntityListener(Family.all
            (PlayerComponent.class).get(), this);
        }    @Override
        public void entityAdded(Entity entity) {
            player = entity;
            playerComponent =
            entity.getComponent(PlayerComponent.class);
            characterComponent =
            entity.getComponent(CharacterComponent.class);
            modelComponent = entity.getComponent(ModelComponent.class);
        }
        @Override
        public void update(float delta) {
            if (player == null) return;
            updateMovement(delta);
        }
        private void updateMovement(float delta) {
            float deltaX = -Gdx.input.getDeltaX() * 0.5f;
            float deltaY = -Gdx.input.getDeltaY() * 0.5f;
            tmp.set(0, 0, 0);
            camera.rotate(camera.up, deltaX);
            tmp.set(camera.direction).crs(camera.up).nor();
            camera.direction.rotate(tmp, deltaY);
            //Move
            Matrix4 ghost = new Matrix4();
            Vector3 translation = new Vector3();
            characterComponent.ghostObject.getWorldTransform(ghost);
            ghost.getTranslation(translation);
            modelComponent.instance.transform.set(translation.x,
            translation.y, translation.z, camera.direction.x,
            camera.direction.y, camera.direction.z, 0);
            camera.position.set(translation.x, translation.y,
            translation.z);
            camera.update(true);
        }
        ...
    }
```

The movement requires some math. First, we will set the characterDirection vector to
$1, 0, 0$, which makes it rotate along the x axis. Then, we will rotate it with the transform of
the model. Once that's done, we will reset the walkDirection vector. Then, we will poll
whether the **W** or the **S** key is pressed, and add or subtract the camera direction to the
walkDirection vector. Then we will poll for the **A** and **D** key, which is to move sideways.

If one of them is pressed, we will set the `tmp` vector to the cross-product of the `camera.direction` and the `camera.up` vector, which is then added to the `walkDirection`. Then, we will scale the `walkDirection` vector with a speed and the `delta` time. Lastly, we will set the `characterController` class' `walkDirection` to the one we just calculated, as shown in the following code snippet:

```
characterComponent.characterDirection.set(-1, 0,
0).rot(modelComponent.instance.transform);
        characterComponent.walkDirection.set(0, 0, 0);
        if (Gdx.input.isKeyPressed(Input.Keys.W))
        characterComponent.walkDirection.add(camera.direction);
        if (Gdx.input.isKeyPressed(Input.Keys.S))
        characterComponent.walkDirection.sub(camera.direction);
        tmp.set(0, 0, 0);
        if (Gdx.input.isKeyPressed(Input.Keys.A))
        tmp.set(camera.direction).crs(camera.up).nor().scl(-1);
        if (Gdx.input.isKeyPressed(Input.Keys.D))
        tmp.set(camera.direction).crs(camera.up).nor().scl(1);
        characterComponent.walkDirection.add(tmp);
        characterComponent.walkDirection.scl(10f * delta);
characterComponent.characterController.setWalkDirection(characterComponent.
walkDirection);
```

Lastly, we would like the camera position to be set to the player so that it becomes first person. This can be done with the following code snippet:

```
camera.position.set(translation.x, translation.y, translation.z);
camera.update(true);
//The update method is now the following
private void updateMovement(float delta) {
    float deltaX = -Gdx.input.getDeltaX() * 0.5f;
    float deltaY = -Gdx.input.getDeltaY() * 0.5f;
    tmp.set(0, 0, 0);
    camera.rotate(camera.up, deltaX);
    tmp.set(camera.direction).crs(camera.up).nor();
    camera.direction.rotate(tmp, deltaY);
    tmp.set(0, 0, 0);
    characterComponent.characterDirection.set(-1, 0,
0).rot(modelComponent.instance.transform).nor();
    characterComponent.walkDirection.set(0, 0, 0);
    if (Gdx.input.isKeyPressed(Input.Keys.W))
    characterComponent.walkDirection.add(camera.direction);
    if (Gdx.input.isKeyPressed(Input.Keys.S))
    characterComponent.walkDirection.sub(camera.direction);
    if (Gdx.input.isKeyPressed(Input.Keys.A))
    tmp.set(camera.direction).crs(camera.up).scl(-1);
    if (Gdx.input.isKeyPressed(Input.Keys.D))
```

```
    tmp.set(camera.direction).crs(camera.up);
    characterComponent.walkDirection.add(tmp);
    characterComponent.walkDirection.scl(10f * delta);
characterComponent.characterController.setWalkDirection(characterComponent.
walkDirection);
    Matrix4 ghost = new Matrix4();
    Vector3 translation = new Vector3();
    characterComponent.ghostObject.getWorldTransform(ghost);    //TODO export
this
    ghost.getTranslation(translation);
    modelComponent.instance.transform.set(translation.x,
    translation.y,
    translation.z, camera.direction.x, camera.direction.y,
    camera.direction.z,
    0);
    camera.position.set(translation.x, translation.y, translation.z);
    camera.update(true);
}
//Now adding it to the GameWorld:
public class GameWorld {
    ...
    private Entity character;


...
private void initPersCamera() {
        perspectiveCamera = new PerspectiveCamera(FOV, Core.VIRTUAL_WIDTH,
        Core.VIRTUAL_HEIGHT);
    }

    private void addEntities() {
        ...
        createPlayer(5, 3, 5);
    }

    private void createPlayer(float x, float y, float z) {
        character = EntityFactory.createPlayer(bulletSystem, x, y,
        z);
        engine.addEntity(character);
    }

    private void addSystems() {
        ...
        engine.addSystem(new PlayerSystem(this, perspectiveCamera));
    }

    public void dispose() {
        bulletSystem.collisionWorld.removeAction(character.getComponent
        (CharacterComponent.class).characterController);
```

```
        bulletSystem.collisionWorld.removeCollisionObject
        (character.getComponent(CharacterComponent.class).ghostObject);
        character.getComponent(CharacterComponent.class)
        .characterController.dispose();
        character.getComponent(CharacterComponent.class)
        .ghostObject.dispose();
        character.getComponent(CharacterComponent.class)
        .ghostShape.dispose();
        ...
    }
}
```

A few additions to the class. We will add the `Entity` global field for the character, then clean up the `initPersCamera`, and leave only the constructor of the camera. On the `addEntities`, we will create a new method called `createPlayer`, which will take its position in the world. This new method calls the previously created `createPlayer` from the `EntityFactory` class, and finally `createPlayer` will add the character entity to the system with `addEntity`.

On the `addSystems` method, we will get to add `PlayerSystem`, and on the `dispose` method, we will have new things to call with regards to the shapes, objects, and others from the player entity.

Run it and you should see this, and you should also be able to move:

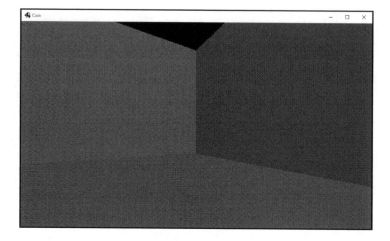

Neat! Let's add enemies now.

Adding enemies

In order to add the finishing touch to our world prototype, we'll need a small gameplay prototype. This will consist of enemies spawning randomly around in our world. For now, it is quite a simple class; however; we should be prepared to upgrade it to a more complex algorithm in the future.

Enemy component

The enemy component is a simple one that contains three different behavior types, such as idle, fleeing, and hunting. We won't differentiate between these right now; however, these three states will determine how an enemy acts and reacts in the future:

```
public class EnemyComponent extends Component {
    public enum STATE {
        IDLE,
        FLEEING,
        HUNTING
    }
    public STATE state = STATE.IDLE;
    public EnemyComponent(STATE state){
        this.state = state;
    }
}
```

Status component

Another component that we will need is a status component. This component holds one Boolean to determine whether the entity is alive or dead. If the entity is dead, it should be removed from the system and a new enemy should be spawned, as shown in the following code snippet:

```
public class StatusComponent extends Component{
    public boolean alive;
    public StatusComponent(){
        alive = true;
    }
}
//Now we are able to spawn an enemy with the following creation function:
public static Entity createEnemy(BulletSystem bulletSystem, float x, float
y, float z) {
    Entity entity = createCharacter(bulletSystem, x, y, z);
    entity.add(new EnemyComponent(EnemyComponent.STATE.HUNTING));
```

```
        entity.add(new StatusComponent());
        return entity;
    }
```

Enemy system

The enemy system is the brain of the enemy AI. This system determines the behavior of enemies which, for now, is quite simple—locate the player and move towards him. It is important that you create an empty instance of the `playerPosition` as well as the `enemyPosition` before you call `getTranslation()`. The `getTransaltion()` function will not work if the object is null, as it depends on the properties of the `Vector` object being already set. We won't have to do any 3D math in this class as we are viewing the relative positions of the characters in a plane. Thus, the enemies do not care how high in the air you are, they only care about where you are related to the *x* and *z* axes (the ground). We will determine the delta **X** and delta **Z** and use simple trigonometry to get the angle of approach for the enemy. We want to find an angle between the **Player** and the **Enemy**, as shown in this illustration:

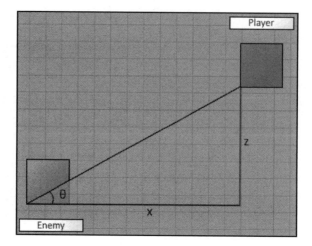

Once we have obtained the angle, we will create a quaternion from it. Based on this quaternion, we can make the enemy look at the player:

```
public class EnemySystem extends EntitySystem implements EntityListener {
    private ImmutableArray<Entity> entities;
    private Entity player;
    private Quaternion quat = new Quaternion();
    private Engine engine;
    private GameWorld gameWorld;
```

```java
ComponentMapper<CharacterComponent> cm =
ComponentMapper.getFor(CharacterComponent.class);
public EnemySystem(GameWorld gameWorld) {
    this.gameWorld = gameWorld;
}
@Override
public void addedToEngine(Engine e) {
    entities = e.getEntitiesFor(Family.all(EnemyComponent.class,
    CharacterComponent.class).get());
    e.addEntityListener(Family.one(PlayerComponent.class).get(), this);
    this.engine = e;
}
public void update(float delta) {
    if (entities.size() < 1) {
        Random random = new Random();
        engine.addEntity(EntityFactory.createEnemy
        (gameWorld.bulletSystem,
        random.nextInt(40) - 20, 10, random.nextInt(40) - 20));
    }

    for (Entity e : entities) {
        ModelComponent mod =
        e.getComponent(ModelComponent.class);
        ModelComponent playerModel =
        player.getComponent(ModelComponent.class);
        Vector3 playerPosition = new Vector3();
        Vector3 enemyPosition = new Vector3();
        playerPosition =
        playerModel.instance.transform.getTranslation(playerPosition);
        enemyPosition =
        mod.instance.transform.getTranslation(enemyPosition);
        float dX = playerPosition.x - enemyPosition.x;
        float dZ = playerPosition.z - enemyPosition.z;
        float theta = (float) (Math.atan2(dX, dZ));
        //Calculate the transforms
        Quaternion rot = quat.setFromAxis(0, 1, 0, (float)
        Math.toDegrees(theta) + 90);
        // Walk
        Matrix4 ghost = new Matrix4();
        Vector3 translation = new Vector3();
        cm.get(e).ghostObject.getWorldTransform(ghost);
        ghost.getTranslation(translation);
        mod.instance.transform.set(translation.x, translation.y,
        translation.z, rot.x, rot.y, rot.z, rot.w);
    }
}
@Override
public void entityAdded(Entity entity) {
```

```
        player = entity;
    }
    @Override
    public void entityRemoved(Entity entity) {
    }
}
```

Now that the enemy has the correct angle, it will still need to move to the player! For this, we will set the `characterDirection` and the `walkDirection` vector. The character will move towards the `characterDirection` with a speed of `walkDirection`.

This is a simplified version of what the player uses:

```
cm.get(e).characterDirection.set(-1, 0, 0).rot(mod.instance.transform);
cm.get(e).walkDirection.set(0, 0, 0);
cm.get(e).walkDirection.add(cm.get(e).characterDirection);
cm.get(e).walkDirection.scl(3f * delta);
cm.get(e).characterController.setWalkDirection(cm.get(e).walkDirection);
```

Once these five lines are added to the update function, the enemy should be able to move!

Enemy collision

There is one last thing to do now that the enemy will walk towards the player and the player can move. Nothing happens when the enemy and player collide!

This has to be done in `BulletSystem`. A custom contact listener is needed; this can be done by creating a new class and enabling it. In the contact listener, we will override the method that is being called when a collision occurs, the `onContactStarted` method. In this method, we will first see if both the collision objects contain an entity in the user data. When that's the case, we will determine if one of them is the player and the other is the enemy. If the player and the enemy collide, we will decrease the health of the player and destroy the enemy by setting the `alive` flag to `false`:

```
public class MyContactListener extends ContactListener {
    @Override
    public void onContactStarted(btCollisionObject colObj0,
    btCollisionObject
    colObj1){
        if (colObj0.userData instanceof Entity && colObj1.userData
        instanceof
        Entity) {
            Entity entity0 = (Entity) colObj0.userData;
            Entity entity1 = (Entity) colObj1.userData;
            if (entity0.getComponent(CharacterComponent.class) !=
```

```
            null &&
            entity1.getComponent(CharacterComponent.class) != null)
            {
                if (entity0.getComponent(EnemyComponent.class) !=
                null) {
                    if
                    (entity0.getComponent
                    (StatusComponent.class).alive)
                    entity1.getComponent
                    (PlayerComponent.class).health -= 10;
                    entity0.getComponent
                    (StatusComponent.class).alive =
                        false;
                } else {
                    if (entity1.getComponent
                        (StatusComponent.class).alive)
                        entity0.getComponent
                        (PlayerComponent.class).health -= 10;
                    entity1.getComponent
                    (StatusComponent.class).alive =
                    false;
                }
            }
        }
    }
}
```

This class now has to be used. In the `BulletSystem` constructor, add the following:

```
public BulletSystem() {
    MyContactListener myContactListener = new MyContactListener();
    myContactListener.enable();      ... }
```

This will ensure that the custom contact listener is being used.

We will now need a new class called `StatusSystem` to check for enemy statuses:

```
public class StatusSystem extends EntitySystem {
    private ImmutableArray<Entity> entities;
    private GameWorld gameWorld;

    public StatusSystem(GameWorld gameWorld) {
        this.gameWorld = gameWorld;
    }

    @Override
    public void addedToEngine(Engine engine) {
        entities =
```

```
        engine.getEntitiesFor(Family.all(StatusComponent.class).get());
    }

    @Override
    public void update(float deltaTime) {
        Iterator iterator = entities.iterator();
        while(iterator.hasNext()){
            Entity entity = (Entity) iterator.next();
            if(!entity.getComponent(StatusComponent.class).alive){
                gameWorld.remove(entity);
            }
        }
    }
}
```

It's an almost straightforward system. The update method is the one we are concerned as we and check for every entity's StatusComponent; if it's not alive, we will remove it.

Then next step is to add a few things to the GameWorld class:

```
public class GameWorld {

    private void addSystems(/*GameUI gameUI*/) {
        ...
        engine.addSystem(new EnemySystem(this));
        engine.addSystem(new StatusSystem(this));
    }

    public void remove(Entity entity) {
        engine.removeEntity(entity);
        bulletSystem.removeBody(entity);
    }
}
```

We get to add small additions such as the EnemySystem and StatusSystems, and then create a new method called remove that's used in the StatusSystem class as explained earlier.

If we run now, enemies should be spawning and chasing us, and being removed on contact with our player:

Making our player able to shoot

The prototype is taking shape. However, the game is slightly unfair at the moment as the player won't have the possibility to fight back! We will give the player a possibility to shoot. Shooting will be done via ray cast tracing.

A ray cast is a line with a direction and no defined end. With ray cast tracing, we will create a line and follow along the line until it hits a collidable object. We will limit the range of the ray somewhat as the computers will calculate infinitely otherwise. Bullet has ray cast tracing possibilities built in. We will use the `ClosestRayResultCallback` class and also add a local field to our `PlayerSystem`:

```
ClosestRayResultCallback rayTestCB;
```

We will then initialize this in our constructor. The constructor we will use has two arguments that are used to define the dimensions of:

```
rayTestCB = new ClosestRayResultCallback(Vector3.Zero, Vector3.Z);.
```

In order to save performance, we will choose to have two new `Vector3` fields; one where the ray starts and another where it ends:

```
Vector3 rayFrom = new Vector3();
Vector3 rayTo = new Vector3();
```

Now, we can start with the `fire` function. First, we will create a ray. We will use a camera for the position and angle of the ray. Then, we will set our `rayTestCB` variables to the ray we just created, and give our ray test a range of 50. Otherwise, it will never stop checking. Then, we will access our collision world and run our raycast tracing test on there. If there is a hit, we will check what kind of object it is. If it is an enemy, indeed, we will kill it by setting its `alive` variable to `false`. Later on, we may also want to keep track of some score:

```
private void fire() {
    Ray ray = camera.getPickRay(Gdx.graphics.getWidth() / 2,
    Gdx.graphics.getHeight() / 2);
    rayFrom.set(ray.origin);
    rayTo.set(ray.direction).scl(50f).add(rayFrom); /* 50 meters max from
the
    origin*/
    /* Because we reuse the ClosestRayResultCallback, we need reset it's
values*/
    rayTestCB.setCollisionObject(null);
    rayTestCB.setClosestHitFraction(1f);
    rayTestCB.setRayFromWorld(rayFrom);
    rayTestCB.setRayToWorld(rayTo);
    gameWorld.bulletSystem.collisionWorld.rayTest(rayFrom, rayTo,
    rayTestCB);
    if (rayTestCB.hasHit()) {
        final btCollisionObject obj =
        rayTestCB.getCollisionObject();
        if (((Entity)
        obj.userData).getComponent(EnemyComponent.class)
        != null) {
            ((Entity)
        obj.userData).getComponent(StatusComponent.class)
        .alive = false;
        }
    }
}
```

Whenever the user clicks on the mouse or touches the screen, we will make the player shoot. Later on, we will make it more difficult for the player with shooting speed and ammunition. However, for our prototype it won't matter too much yet:

```
private void updateMovement(float delta) {
...     if (Gdx.input.justTouched()) fire();
}
```

Scene2D

Every game has information that the player needs to know, and LibGDX tackles this with an API called **Scene2D** to help us develop and manage the UI with easy, clean, and powerful implementations.

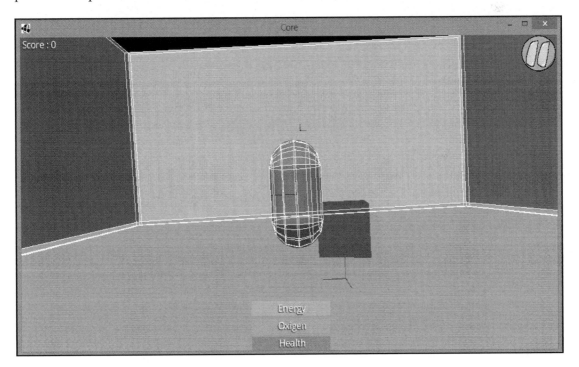

The preceding image is an example of the UI for our game. It's displaying the **Score** (top left), a **Health** bar, an **Oxigen** bar, and an **Energy** bar (bottom middle), and a pause button (top right).

Scene2D is LibGDX's scene graph; its basically, a scene where actors play. It consists of scenes that contain nods and can contain them on various layers. The benefit of using this approach is based on **performance**, **productivity**, **portability**, and **scalability**.

Using Scene2D is as simple as instantiating a `Stage` class and adding actors to it.

We'll start with creating a class that will handle all UI draws and changes; we'll add what we need on `GameScreen.java` first:

```java
public class GameScreen implements Screen {
    ...
    GameUI gameUI;
    public GameScreen(Core game) {
        ...
        gameUI = new GameUI(game);
        gameWorld = new GameWorld(gameUI);
        Settings.Paused = false;
        Gdx.input.setInputProcessor(gameUI.stage);
        ...
    }
    @Override
    public void render(float delta) {
        /** Updates */
        gameUI.update(delta);
        /** Draw */
        gameWorld.render(delta);
        gameUI.render();
    }
    @Override
    public void resize(int width, int height) {
        gameUI.resize(width, height);
        ...
    }
    @Override
    public void dispose() {
        ...
        gameUI.dispose();
    }
}
```

We'll add a new global variable called GameUI that will control all of our UI. In the constructor, we'll add our new GameUI instance, which will receive the app as a parameter, above the line of the GameWorld class' new instance, and now the GameWorld class' constructor will also receive the GameUI instance as a parameter. We will use this instance to pass the status of our player.

Continuing with the GameScreen class' constructor, we will set up the input processor to gameUI.stage, which is the stage inside our gameUI that will hold and control our UI widgets.

With render(), we will set up the respective methods for updates and renders, thereby setting up the gameUI.update(delta) between an if clause that reads our new static Boolean Settings.Paused, and then rendering our UI below the game world (otherwise, the 3D world will be drawn over the UI).

We set up the resize and dispose methods as we did with the game world.

For now, open GameWorld.java and only add the new GameUI class' variable in the constructor.

We'll create a new class called Settings.java, placed on the default package, to set the public static boolean variable called Paused, which we added to the GameScreen class constructor. It will tell us if the player opened the pause dialog:

```java
public class Settings {
    public static boolean Paused;
}
/*Now create a class named GameUI.java and place it on a new package called
UI:*/
public class GameUI {
    private Core game;
    public Stage stage;
    public HealthWidget healthWidget;
    private ScoreWidget scoreWidget;
    private PauseWidget pauseWidget;
    private CrosshairWidget crosshairWidget;
    public GameOverWidget gameOverWidget;
    public GameUI(Core game) {
        this.game = game;
        stage = new Stage(new FitViewport(Core.VIRTUAL_WIDTH,
        Core.VIRTUAL_HEIGHT));
        setWidgets();
        configureWidgets();
    }
    public void setWidgets() {
```

```
            healthWidget = new HealthWidget();
            scoreWidget = new ScoreWidget();
            pauseWidget = new PauseWidget(game, stage);
            crosshairWidget = new CrosshairWidget();
            gameOverWidget = new GameOverWidget(game, stage);
        }
    public void configureWidgets() {
        healthWidget.setSize(140, 25);
        healthWidget.setPosition(Core.VIRTUAL_WIDTH / 2 -
        healthWidget.getWidth() / 2, 0);
        scoreWidget.setSize(140, 25);
        scoreWidget.setPosition(0, Core.VIRTUAL_HEIGHT -
        scoreWidget.getHeight());
        pauseWidget.setSize(64, 64);
        pauseWidget.setPosition(Core.VIRTUAL_WIDTH -
        pauseWidget.getWidth(),
        Core.VIRTUAL_HEIGHT - pauseWidget.getHeight());
        gameOverWidget.setSize(280, 100);
        gameOverWidget.setPosition(Core.VIRTUAL_WIDTH / 2 - 280 / 2,
        Core.VIRTUAL_HEIGHT / 2);
        crosshairWidget.setPosition(Core.VIRTUAL_WIDTH / 2 - 16,
        Core.VIRTUAL_HEIGHT / 2 - 16);
        crosshairWidget.setSize(32, 32);
        stage.addActor(healthWidget);
        stage.addActor(scoreWidget);
        stage.addActor(crosshairWidget);
        stage.setKeyboardFocus(pauseWidget);
    }
    public void update(float delta) {
        stage.act(delta);
    }
    public void render() {
        stage.draw();
    }
    public void resize(int width, int height) {
        stage.getViewport().update(width, height);
    }
    public void dispose() {
        stage.dispose();
    }
}
```

This class will handle the UI renders and its updates. It contains a `Stage` class and its actors, which are the widgets (`HealthWidget`, `ScoreWidget`, and so on).

In the constructor, we will grab an instance of our game and initialize the Stage class with a FitViewport and our main width and height; this will also scale and maintain the aspect ratio, that is, our screen to any size that we'd like or the current device's size where the game is being played. Then, we will set the widgets on a separate method called setWidgets(), Health, Score, Pause, Crosshair, and GameOver. Pause and GameOver widgets will take as constructors the game and stage.

In configureWidgets(), we'll set their sizes and positions, and add them to the actual stage and this last one will render them; however, the GameOverWidget and PauseWidget will not be added right now. They will add themselves to listen to key presses. We will also need to set the focus to PauseWidget to listen to the escape presses *(Esc)* on the keyboard.

On separate methods, add the update, render, dispose, and resize methods where we'll call our Stage to configure itself, and do the heavy weight on each.

Default skin for Scene2D

In order to use Scene2D, we will need to load a skin file for the widgets to use for draws. LibGDX comes with a default that we need to setup manually. We will do that now. Download the default skin from our repository (https://github.com/DeeepGames/SpaceG ladiators) on android/assets/data, and the files you will need are:

```
uiskin.png
uiskin.json
uiskin.atlas
default.png
default.fnt
```

Place the files in the Android project, in the folder assets/data (create directory data).

Now, add the constructor to Core.java and its dispose method:

```
public class Core extends ApplicationAdapter {
    ...
    @Override
    public void create() {
        new Assets();
        ...
    }
    ...
    @Override
    public void dispose() {
        Assets.dispose();
```

```
        }
    }
```

Let's create a new file called `Assets.java` and place it in the default package:

```
public class Assets {
    public static Skin skin;
    public Assets() {
        skin = new Skin();
        FileHandle fileHandle =
        Gdx.files.internal("data/uiskin.json");
        FileHandle atlasFile = fileHandle.sibling("uiskin.atlas");
        if (atlasFile.exists()) {
            skin.addRegions(new TextureAtlas(atlasFile));
        }
        skin.load(fileHandle);
    }
    public static void dispose() {
        skin.dispose();
    }
}
```

`Assets.java` will start adding a `public static Skin` variable that can be accessed from all parts of our game; we will need that.

The constructor will initialize this `Skin`; then load configuration file; load the atlas; and then add all the regions to the skin. Then, when the app is closed, we'll dispose the skin.

This is all we need to set up the default skin. This default skin comes with everything we will need for a prototype and uses any of the widgets available; this is all we will need for now. Now, we'll move to use it.

Health bar

We'll create our health widget class that will handle all the changes on the health of our player and also render itself on our UI camera contained on the stage.

For this, we will need to create a class called `HealthWidget.java` and place it in a new package called `widgets`:

```
public class HealthWidget extends Actor {
    private ProgressBar healthBar;
    private ProgressBar.ProgressBarStyle progressBarStyle;
    private Label label;
    public HealthWidget() {
```

```
        progressBarStyle = new ProgressBar.ProgressBarStyle(
                Assets.skin.newDrawable("white", Color.RED),
                Assets.skin.newDrawable("white", Color.GREEN));
                progressBarStyle.knobBefore = progressBarStyle.knob;
                healthBar = new ProgressBar(0, 100, 1, false,
                progressBarStyle);
                label = new Label("Health", Assets.skin);
                label.setAlignment(Align.center);
        }
    @Override
    public void act(float delta) {
        healthBar.act(delta);
        label.act(delta);
    }
    @Override
    public void draw(Batch batch, float parentAlpha) {
        healthBar.draw(batch, parentAlpha);
        label.draw(batch, parentAlpha);
    }
    @Override
    public void setPosition(float x, float y) {
        super.setPosition(x, y);
        healthBar.setPosition(x, y);
        label.setPosition(x, y);
    }
    @Override
    public void setSize(float width, float height) {
        super.setSize(width, height);
        healthBar.setSize(width, height);
        progressBarStyle.background.setMinWidth(width);
        progressBarStyle.background.setMinHeight(height);
        progressBarStyle.knob.setMinWidth(healthBar.getValue());
        progressBarStyle.knob.setMinHeight(height);
        label.setSize(width, height);
    }
    public void setValue(float value) {
        healthBar.setValue(value);
    }
}
```

This class will have `ProgressBar`, `ProgressBarStyle`, and `Label`. It needs to extend an `Actor` class in order to be able to add it to the `Stage` class.

The constructor will initialize the `progressBarStyle` variable with a white image (which is just a white pixel) contained on the default LibGDX's `Skin` class, and we'll tint it with a red color for the background and green for the knob. Next, with that same `progressBarStyle`, we will set the `knobBefore` drawable to be the same knob so as to get a feeling of fill to the right.

Next, we will initialize the `ProgressBar` called `healthBar`—with parameters minimum 0, maximum 100, `stepSize` as 20, vertical `false`—and style our customized `ProgressBarStyle`. We will then set the value of this bar to its maximum, 100.

Next, we will initialize the label with `Health` text and pass it to the `Skin` class from our `Assets`. This method will take the default style for a label and it's assigned on the file `uiskin.json`. And lastly, for the constructor, we'll set the alignment to center.

We will override the `act(...)` method from the `Actor` class to make our progress bar and label update every frame, then override `draw(...)` method to draw them with the `SetPosition()` method for our internal widgets, set its size and set the value of the progress bar to update it on every energy change. Now, open `GameWorld.java` and add:

```
public class GameWorld {
    ...
    public GameWorld(GameUI gameUI) {
        ...
        addSystems(gameUI);
        ...
    }
    ...
    private void addSystems(GameUI gameUI) {
        ...
        engine.addSystem(new PlayerSystem(perspectiveCamera, gameUI,
        engine));
        ...
    }
}
```

Add the `gameUI` variable to the `addSystems()` method and pass the `gameUI` to the `PlayerSystem` constructor. Now, open `PlayerSystem.java` and add:

```
public class PlayerSystem extends EntitySystem implements EntityListener {
    private PlayerComponent playerComponent;
    private GameUI gameUI;
    ...
    public PlayerSystem(Camera camera, GameUI gameUI, Engine engine) {
        ...
        this.gameUI = gameUI;
```

```
    }
    @Override
    public void update(float delta) {
        ...
        updateStatus();
    }
    private void updateStatus() {
        gameUI.healthWidget.setValue(playerComponent.health);
    }
    @Override
    public void entityAdded(Entity entity) {
        ...
        playerComponent =
        entity.getComponent(PlayerComponent.class);
    }
}
```

Now, we'll save an instance of gameUI and add a new method called updateStatus() inside update(), and inside this new method, we will set the health of the player on every frame of the UI.

The entityAdded() method will now save the playerComponent variable that the actual player brings, when it's added to the engine, and with this, we can get the health and add it to the UI. This is all we will need to display health.

Crosshair

We will now want to add a simple crosshair to make the shooting easier. Let's create a new class called CrosshairWidget.java, make it extend Actor, and place it in the UI package:

```
public class CrosshairWidget extends Actor {
    private Image crosshairDot, crosshairInnerRing;
    public CrosshairWidget() {
        crosshairDot = new Image(new
        Texture(Gdx.files.internal("crosshair/crossHairPoint.png")));
        crosshairInnerRing = new Image(new
        Texture(Gdx.files.internal("crosshair/crossHairInnerRing.png")));
    }
    @Override
    public void act(float delta) {
        if (Settings.Paused) return;
    }
    @Override
    public void draw(Batch batch, float parentAlpha) {
        if (Settings.Paused) return;
```

```
        crosshairDot.draw(batch, parentAlpha);
        crosshairInnerRing.draw(batch, parentAlpha);
    }
    @Override
    public void setPosition(float x, float y) {
        super.setPosition(x, y);
        crosshairDot.setPosition(x - 16, y - 16);
        crosshairInnerRing.setPosition(x - 16, y - 16);
        crosshairInnerRing.setOrigin(crosshairInnerRing.getWidth() /
        2,
        crosshairInnerRing.getHeight() / 2);
        Logger.log(Logger.ANDREAS, Logger.INFO, "Setting origin to "
        + x + ",
        " + y);
    }
    @Override
    public void setSize(float width, float height) {
        super.setSize(width, height);
        crosshairDot.setSize(width * 2, height * 2);
        crosshairInnerRing.setSize(width * 2, height * 2);
    }
}
```

The code should, at this point, be self-explanatory; we will simply have two sprites on the screen with one point in the center and a ring around it. We will set the origin in the `setPosition` function in order to make it the center of the sprite. This is useful if you want to make the ring rotate around the point that we experimented with.

Displaying scores

Now that we can kill enemies, we want to save our score and add a bit of a challenge to compete with friends. We'll start by creating the widget to handle this, `ScoreWidget.java`:

```
public class ScoreWidget extends Actor {
    Label label;
    public ScoreWidget() {
        label = new Label("", Assets.skin);
    }
    @Override
    public void act(float delta) {
        label.act(delta);
        label.setText("Score : " + PlayerComponent.score);
    }
    @Override
    public void draw(Batch batch, float parentAlpha) {
        label.draw(batch, parentAlpha);
```

```
    }
    @Override
    public void setPosition(float x, float y) {
        super.setPosition(x, y);
        label.setPosition(x, y);
    }
    @Override
    public void setSize(float width, float height) {
        super.setSize(width, height);
        label.setSize(width, height);
    }
}
```

As usual for the widgets, we will start by extending `Actor` on the class. This widget will only need one Scene2D widget: a label. For our prototype concerns, it's enough.

Instantiate it in the constructor, override the `draw`, `setSize`, `setPosition`, and `act` methods; however, on this last one, we'll set the label's text to the actual score, that is, a static variable on the `PlayerComponent` class and `PlayerComponent.score`. Now, open `PlayerComponent.java` and add:

```
public class PlayerComponent extends Component {
    ...
    public static int score;
    public PlayerComponent() {
        ...
        score = 0;
    }
}
```

Now, open `PlayerSystem.java` and add:

```
public class PlayerSystem extends EntitySystem implements EntityListener {
    ...
    private void fire() {
        ...
        if (rayTestCB.hasHit()) {
            final btCollisionObject obj = rayTestCB.getCollisionObject();
            if (((Entity) obj.userData).getComponent(EnemyComponent.class) !=
            null) {
                ((Entity)
                obj.userData).getComponent(StatusComponent.class).alive =
                false;
                PlayerComponent.score += 100;
            }
        }
```

```
    }
    ...
}
```

This is where we will add the score when killing an enemy. That is all that we will need to display the current score. At this point, with everything together, it should look like this:

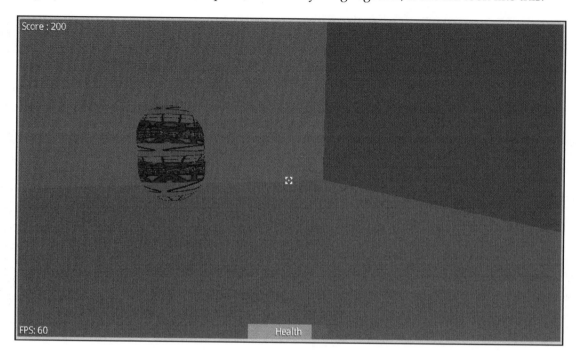

Pausing the game

A new widget called PauseWidget.java will do a bit more work than the others; we'll start with creating the class, PauseWidget.java, and place it in the UI package:

```
public class PauseWidget extends Actor {
    private Core game;
    private Window window;
    private TextButton closeDialog, restartButton, quitButton;
    private Stage stage;
    public PauseWidget(Core game, Stage stage) {
        this.game = game;
        this.stage = stage;
        setWidgets();
        configureWidgets();
```

```
        setListeners();
    }
    private void setWidgets() {
        window = new Window("Pause", Assets.skin);
        closeDialog = new TextButton("X", Assets.skin);
        restartButton = new TextButton("Restart", Assets.skin);
        quitButton = new TextButton("Quit", Assets.skin);
    }
    private void configureWidgets() {
        window.getTitleTable().add(closeDialog).height
        (window.getPadTop());
        window.add(restartButton);
        window.add(quitButton);
    }

    private void setListeners() {
        super.addListener(new InputListener() {
            @Override
            public boolean keyDown(InputEvent event, int keycode) {
                if (keycode == Input.Keys.ESCAPE) {
                    handleUpdates();
                    return true;
                }
                return false;
            }
        });
        closeDialog.addListener(new ClickListener() {
            @Override
            public void clicked(InputEvent inputEvent, float x,
            float y) {
                handleUpdates();
            }
        });
        restartButton.addListener(new ClickListener() {
            @Override
            public void clicked(InputEvent inputEvent, float x,
            float y) {
                game.setScreen(new GameScreen(game));
            }
        });
        quitButton.addListener(new ClickListener() {
            @Override
            public void clicked(InputEvent inputEvent, float x,
            float y) {
                Gdx.app.exit();
            }
        });
    }
```

```
        private void handleUpdates() {
            if (window.getStage() == null) {
                stage.addActor(window);
                Gdx.input.setCursorCatched(false);
                Settings.Paused = true;
            } else {
                window.remove();
                Gdx.input.setCursorCatched(true);
                Settings.Paused = false;
            }
        }
        @Override
        public void setPosition(float x, float y) {
            super.setPosition(x, y);
            window.setPosition(Core.VIRTUAL_WIDTH / 2 -
            window.getWidth() / 2,
            Core.VIRTUAL_HEIGHT / 2 - window.getHeight() / 2);
        }
        @Override
        public void setSize(float width, float height) {
            super.setSize(width, height);
            window.setSize(width * 2, height * 2);
        }
    }
```

A bit more complex than the other widgets so far, we will start with saving the `game` and `stage` instances in the constructor because we will need them.

Initialize on `setWidgets()`, then configure and add the respective widgets to the window we just created on `configureWidgets()`.

On the `addListeners()` method, the thing gets a bit confusing as we want to press *Esc* on the keyboard and pause the game. The `InputListener` class will read the keycode passed and check if it's *Esc* and then handle the update. For the rest of the buttons, they will all implement the `ClickListener` class but will have different functions, of course. The `closeDialog` textbutton will just call `handleUpdates()`, `restartButton` will set a new GameScreen, and the `quitButton` will call `Gdx.app.exit()`.

Let's create a `private void` method called `handleUpdates` now. This one will read if the window widget has a stage already set, if not, it will add it. Then, it will set the cursor `catched` to `false`, so as to see the cursor again; and finally, set the Boolean pause to `true`. If our window does have a stage set, it will do the opposite. The rest of the methods will do regular stuff that all widgets do.

Our working widget will look like this:

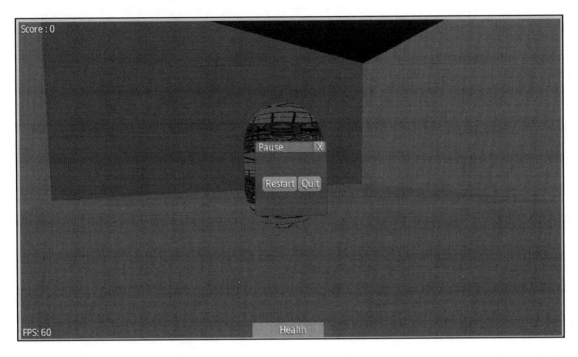

But this won't pause the game just yet. In order to get this widget to work correctly, we will need to set the Settings.Paused Boolean on the necessary places. Fire up GameWorld.java and add:

```java
public class GameWorld {
    ...
    public void render(float delta) {
        ...
        checkPause();
    }
    private void checkPause() {
        if (Settings.Paused) {
            movementSystem.setProcessing(false);
            playerSystem.setProcessing(false);
            collisionSystem.setProcessing(false);
        } else {
            movementSystem.setProcessing(true);
            playerSystem.setProcessing(true);
            collisionSystem.setProcessing(true);
        }
    }
}
```

Now, the `render()` method will include a new method called `checkPause()`. This method will read `Settings.Paused` value and set the processing of the systems to `false` or `true`, depending on the value. This will make a game paused effect when we open the pause dialog.

Game over widget

Our next widget, and the last for our prototype, is the game over widget. Let's create `GameOverWidget.java` and do this:

```
public class GameOverWidget extends Actor {
    private Core game;
    private Stage stage;
    private Image image;
    private TextButton retryB, leaderB, quitB;
    public GameOverWidget(Core game, Stage stage) {
        this.game = game;
        this.stage = stage;
        setWidgets();
        setListeners();
    }
    private void setWidgets() {
        image = new Image(new
        Texture(Gdx.files.internal("data/gameOver.png")));
        retryB = new TextButton("Retry", Assets.skin);
        leaderB = new TextButton("Leaderboards", Assets.skin);
        quitB = new TextButton("Quit", Assets.skin);
    }

    private void setListeners() {
        retryB.addListener(new ClickListener() {
            @Override
            public void clicked(InputEvent event, float x, float y)
            {
                game.setScreen(new GameScreen(game));
            }
        });
        leaderB.addListener(new ClickListener() {
            @Override
            public void clicked(InputEvent event, float x, float y)
            {
                game.setScreen(new LeaderboardsScreen(game));
            }
        });
        quitB.addListener(new ClickListener() {
```

```
            @Override
            public void clicked(InputEvent event, float x, float y)
            {
                Gdx.app.exit();
            }
        });
    }
    @Override
    public void setPosition(float x, float y) {
        super.setPosition(0, 0);
        image.setPosition(x, y + 32);
        retryB.setPosition(x - 45, y - 96);
        leaderB.setPosition(x + retryB.getWidth() - 25, y - 96);
        quitB.setPosition(x + retryB.getWidth() +
        leaderB.getWidth(), y - 96);
    }
    @Override
    public void setSize(float width, float height) {
        super.setSize(Core.VIRTUAL_WIDTH, Core.VIRTUAL_HEIGHT);
        image.setSize(width, height);
        retryB.setSize(width / 2.5f, height / 2);
        leaderB.setSize(width / 2.5f, height / 2);
        quitB.setSize(width / 2.5f, height / 2);
    }
    public void gameOver() {
        stage.addActor(image);
        stage.addActor(retryB);
        stage.addActor(leaderB);
        stage.addActor(quitB);
        stage.unfocus(stage.getKeyboardFocus());
        Gdx.input.setCursorCatched(false);
    }
}
```

The regular class, as with the other widgets, is more similar to the Pause widget.

It saves an instance of the game, the stage, and the set widgets and sets the game over image with the one we made (again, from our repository, gameOver.png (https://github .com/DeeepGames/SpaceGladiators), or make your own).

The SetPosition() will have some magic numbers to set the layout of this widget so take good care of them.

The real deal on this widget is the public method: gameOver(). This one will add all the actors inside these widgets to the stage once the player reaches to zero health. It will also take away the keyboard focus of the stage so we can't open the pause window again. Then it will set the cursor catched to false. To call this last method, we'll need to have the widget set to public modifier and the method too.

Now, open up PlayerSystem.java and add the following:

```
public class PlayerSystem extends EntitySystem implements EntityListener {
    ...
    @Override
    public void update(float delta) {
        ...
        checkGameOver();
    }
    ...
    private void checkGameOver() {
        if (playerComponent.health <= 0 && !Settings.Paused) {
            Settings.Pause = true;
            gameUI.gameOverWidget.gameOver();
        }
    }
    ...
}
```

The Update() method from PlayerSystem.java will now include checkGameOver(). This new method will check if the player's health is below or equal to zero and Pause the variable if false. It will set Pause to true and call our newly created method on our widget. It should now look like this:

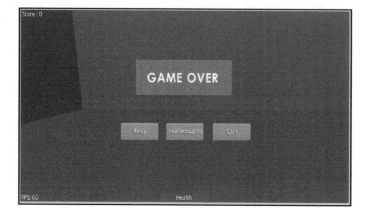

Screens

We already have a screen that renders the game, and all it needs to work and have gameplay. Now, we will need to add other common screens (unless you go with an original design). For our game, we'll need: a main menu screen, a loading screen (to avoid weird freezes), and a leaderboards screen.

Main menu screen

Our main menu screen needs to have some basic items such as a background, a title, a play button, a leaderboards button, and a quit button. We won't get into more details because we are building a prototype so we'll only include the primary features.

We will first change `Core.java` to make it read our main menu screen before launching the actual game screen:

```
Core.java to make it read our main menu screen before launching the actual
game screen:

public class Core extends ApplicationAdapter {
    ...
    @Override
    public void create() {
        ...
        setScreen(new MainMenuScreen(this));
    }
    ...
}
```

Let's create a class called `MainMenuScreen.java` and place it on our screens package:

```
public class MainMenuScreen implements Screen {
    Core game;
    Stage stage;
    Image backgroundImage, titleImage;
    TextButton playButton, leaderboardsButton, quitButton;
    public MainMenuScreen(Core game) {
        this.game = game;
        stage = new Stage(new FitViewport(Core.VIRTUAL_WIDTH,
        Core.VIRTUAL_HEIGHT));
        setWidgets();
        configureWidgers();
        setListeners();
        Gdx.input.setInputProcessor(stage);
    }
```

```
    private void setWidgets() {
        backgroundImage = new Image(new
        Texture(Gdx.files.internal("data/backgroundMN.png")));
        titleImage = new Image(new
        Texture(Gdx.files.internal("data/title.png")));
        playButton = new TextButton("Play", Assets.skin);
        leaderboardsButton = new TextButton("Leaderboards",
        Assets.skin);
        quitButton = new TextButton("Quit", Assets.skin);
    }
    private void configureWidgers() {
        backgroundImage.setSize(Core.VIRTUAL_WIDTH,
        Core.VIRTUAL_HEIGHT);
        titleImage.setSize(620, 200);
        titleImage.setPosition(Core.VIRTUAL_WIDTH / 2 -
        titleImage.getWidth()
        / 2, Core.VIRTUAL_HEIGHT / 2);
        playButton.setSize(128, 64);
        playButton.setPosition(Core.VIRTUAL_WIDTH / 2 -
        playButton.getWidth()
        / 2, Core.VIRTUAL_HEIGHT / 2 - 100);
        leaderboardsButton.setSize(128, 64);
        leaderboardsButton.setPosition(Core.VIRTUAL_WIDTH / 2 -
        playButton.getWidth() / 2, Core.VIRTUAL_HEIGHT / 2 - 170);
        quitButton.setSize(128, 64);
        quitButton.setPosition(Core.VIRTUAL_WIDTH / 2 -
        playButton.getWidth()
        / 2, Core.VIRTUAL_HEIGHT / 2 - 240);
        stage.addActor(backgroundImage);
        stage.addActor(titleImage);
        stage.addActor(playButton);
        stage.addActor(leaderboardsButton);
        stage.addActor(quitButton);
    }

    private void setListeners() {
        playButton.addListener(new ClickListener() {
            @Override
            public void clicked(InputEvent event, float x, float y) {
                game.setScreen(new GameScreen(game));
            }
        });
        leaderboardsButton.addListener(new ClickListener() {
            @Override
            public void clicked(InputEvent event, float x, float y) {
                game.setScreen(new LeaderboardsScreen(game));
            }
        });
```

```
            quitButton.addListener(new ClickListener() {
                @Override
                public void clicked(InputEvent event, float x, float y) {
                    Gdx.app.exit();
                }
            });
        }
        @Override
        public void render(float delta) {
            /** Updates */
            stage.act(delta);
            /** Draw */
            stage.draw();
        }
        @Override
        public void resize(int width, int height) {
            stage.getViewport().update(width, height);
        }
        @Override
        public void dispose() {
            stage.dispose();
        }
        // empty methods from Screen
    }
```

We'll start implementing the `Screen` interface on our class, because, as you know, this is a screen. We will save a `Core` instance to be a global variable, then create a new `Stage` object that will contain our new widgets for this respective screen, which is a `backgroundImage`, a `titleImage`, a `playButton`, a `leaderboardsButton`, and a `quitButton`.

Let's create a constructor for the class and have a `Core game` parameter to pass by our game instance, then save it. We'll instantiate the `Stage` object with a `FitViewport` again, with our static `VIRTUAL_WIDTH` and `VIRTUAL_HEIGHT` on the `Core` class.

The `SetWidgets()` method again will instantiate our widgets with our resources (skin, images, and font). Configure your widgets on the respective method. Then, we'll set the listeners for when we click the buttons and set the new screen with our game instance.

And finally, we will set our new input processor as the `stage`. Everything else is common code for most screens, such as the `resize`, `render`, and `dispose` methods.

Using the resources we created for this prototype, we should see something like this:

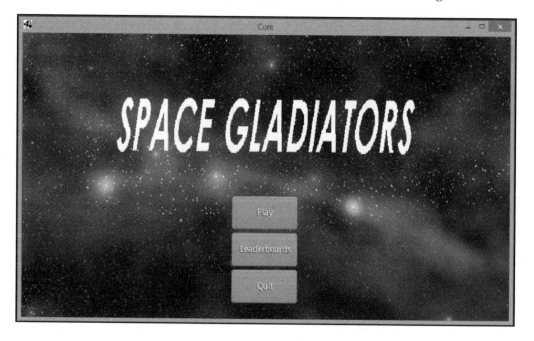

Leaderboards screen and the Settings class

We will add a leaderboards screen on our game, and for this we'll need to save the score in a file after the game is over.

First, we will start adding what we need to create and read the file that will hold our scores, modify `Core.java`, and add the following:

```java
public class Core extends ApplicationAdapter {
    ...
    @Override
    public void create() {
        ...
        new Settings().load();
        ...
    }
    ...
    @Override
    public void dispose() {
        Settings.save();
    }
```

```
}
```

Under the `Assets` instantiation, add the call to the `load()` method.

The `Settings` class will now implement a few new methods:

```
public class Settings {
    ...
    public static boolean soundEnabled = true;
    public static int[] highscores = new int[]{1000, 800, 500, 300, 100};
    public final static String file = ".spaceglad";
    public static void load() {
        try {
            FileHandle filehandle = Gdx.files.external(file);
            String[] strings = filehandle.readString().split("\n");
            soundEnabled = Boolean.parseBoolean(strings[0]);
            for (int i = 0; i < 5; i++) highscores[i] =
            Integer.parseInt(strings[i + 1]);
        } catch (Throwable e) {
        }
    }
    public static void save() {
        try {
            FileHandle filehandle = Gdx.files.external(file);
            filehandle.writeString(Boolean.toString(soundEnabled) +
            "\n",
            false);
            for (int i = 0; i < 5; i++)
            filehandle.writeString(Integer.toString(highscores[i]) +
            "\n",
            true);
        } catch (Throwable e) {
        }
    }
    public static void addScore(int score) {
        for (int i = 0; i < 5; i++) {
            if (highscores[i] < score) {
                for (int j = 4; j > i; j--) highscores[j] =
                    highscores[j - 1];
                highscores[i] = score;
                break;
            }
        }
    }
}
```

Let's start with adding a new `public static Boolean` called `soundEnabled` and set it to `true`. We'll use this flag for, checking if the sound is enabled and whether it will play or not play sounds and music in the future.

A new static array of integers will contain default scores, for our first time of playing.

And a final static `String` will contain the name of our file, in this case is `.spaceglad`.

We'll implement three new methods to handle scores: `load()`, `save()`, and `addScore(...)`; all of them are statics. The `load()` method tries to get this file or else it creates it. It then splits the file in readable strings separated by a line jump, and then starts reading them. We read the first one and see if there's a sound setting already saved, and then, on a `for` loop, it will read the next lines while looking for scores.

The `save()` method will do the same as `load()` but on the opposite direction, saving the scores while playing and settings changed.

The `addScore(..)` method will do the obvious: reading our strings for the high scores, comparing them, and replacing them.

We already added the call for the leaderboards screen on the `MainMenuScreen.java`, now we will need to create our actual `LeaderboardsScreen.java`:

```java
public class LeaderboardsScreen implements Screen {
    Core game;
    Stage stage;
    Image backgroundImage;
    TextButton backButton;
    Label label[];

    public LeaderboardsScreen(Core game) {
        this.game = game;
        stage = new Stage(new FitViewport(Core.VIRTUAL_WIDTH,
        Core.VIRTUAL_HEIGHT));
        setWidgets();
        configureWidgers();
        setListeners();
        Gdx.input.setInputProcessor(stage);
    }

    private void setWidgets() {
        backgroundImage = new Image(new
        Texture(Gdx.files.internal("data/backgroundMN.png")));
        backButton = new TextButton("Back", Assets.skin);
        label = new Label[5];
        for (int i = 0; i < label.length; i++) label[i] = new
```

```
        Label(i + 1 + ")
        " + Settings.highscores[i], Assets.skin);
    }

    private void configureWidgers() {
        backgroundImage.setSize(Core.VIRTUAL_WIDTH,
        Core.VIRTUAL_HEIGHT);
        backButton.setSize(128, 64);
        backButton.setPosition(Core.VIRTUAL_WIDTH -
        backButton.getWidth() - 5,
        5);
        stage.addActor(backgroundImage);
        stage.addActor(backButton);
        int y = 0;
        for (int i = 0; i < label.length; i++) {
            label[i].setFontScale(3);
            label[i].setPosition(15, Core.VIRTUAL_HEIGHT -
            label[i].getHeight() - 25 - y);
            y += 96;
            stage.addActor(label[i]);
        }
    }

    private void setListeners() {
        backButton.addListener(new ClickListener() {
            @Override
            public void clicked(InputEvent event, float x, float y)
            {
                game.setScreen(new MainMenuScreen(game));
            }
        });
    }

    @Override
    public void render(float delta) {
        /** Updates */
        stage.act(delta);
        /** Draw */
        stage.draw();
    }

    @Override
    public void resize(int width, int height) {
        stage.getViewport().update(width, height);
    }

    @Override
    public void dispose() {
```

```
        stage.dispose();
    }
    // empty methods from Screen
}
```

As is normal for screens, we will start implementing `Screen` on the class and implementing the methods for it, then our `Core` instance, `Stage` instance, and `backgroundImage`. This one will have only one `backButton` and a label array, which will contain and draw the high scores.

The constructor is the same as the `MainMenuScreen.java`.

The `SetWidgets()` method will initialize the background image, as usual, the back button, and then the labels with the respective high score, reading them on a `for` loop.

The `CorfigureWidgets()` method will start doing the usual and then set the labels' position, first scaling the fonts (yeah, it will look awful), and then adding them to the stage.

The `SetListeners()` method will set the back button to go back to the main menu.

And now that everything else is the same as the other screens, it should look like this:

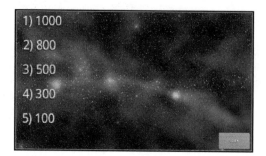

Summary

In this chapter, you learnt how to use basic classes and practices of LibGDX's 3D API, (in addition to Bullet Physics wrapper and Scene2D), all to build a very fancy prototype from scratch.

In the next chapter, we will start preparing the actual visuals and models for our game with the help of Blender, a 3D modeling and general software.

4
Preparing Visuals

In this chapter, we will explain how to create 3D models to import in our game. Creating proper models for our game will help to take it to the next level. Appealing visuals are key in helping the player immerse into the universe of our game. Visuals are key to many games. They help create realistic environments in the case of big AAA games, but they are also crucial to many smaller indie games that follow a specific theme or want the universe to create a specific atmosphere. All of this takes a skilled modeler and animator as well as many man-hours, so for our project we will create some simple models. For this chapter, we will focus on just making the gun for our player.

The following topics will be covered in this chapter:

- Setting up Blender
- Blender basics
- Sketching
- Modeling
- Rigging
- Animating
- Texturing
- Exporting

Setting up Blender

The first thing we need to do is install and set up our work environment to do 3D work, and to achieve this, we simply have to install Blender.

Downloading and installing Blender

Download Blender from the main site (`https://www.blender.org/download/`). The version we are using is 2.75a and you can get it from this link: `http://download.blender.org/release/Blender2.75/`.

Download for the platform you have. Ours is Windows 8.1, 64 bit, and we'll get the MSI installer.

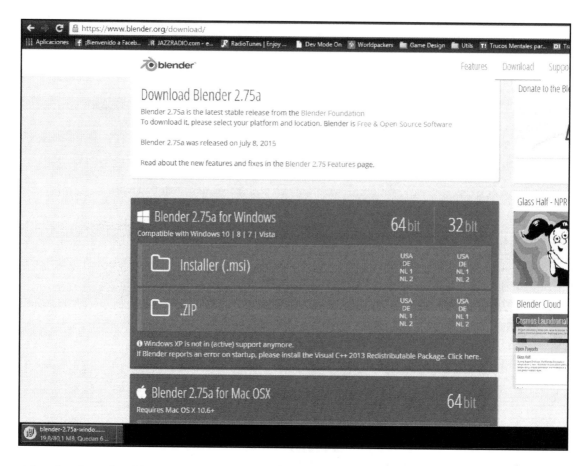

After the download has completed, just execute the installer and put it in your preferred folder.

Blender's (very) basics

Let's start by discussing the very basics of Blender. Interface, shortcuts, buttons, and some of what we see that might be unknown if you have never seen 3D modeling software or any similar modeling software. The very first thing we see, after Blender's introduction, is this:

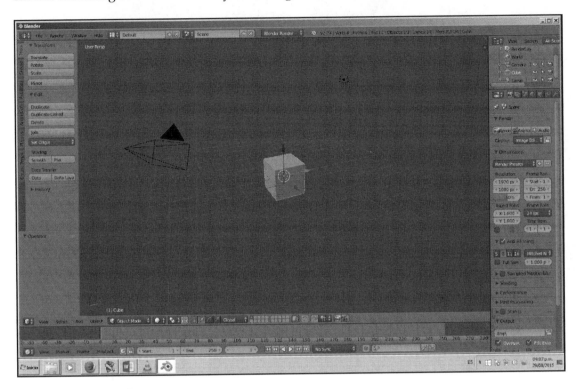

Let's begin by talking about the navigation around the viewport:

- Click the middle button of the mouse (and hold) to rotate the camera around the object.
- Press *Shift* + middle click the mouse button to pan the camera.
- Press *Ctrl* + middle click the mouse button to zoom in and out (you can also use the scrolling wheel).
- With the NumPad we can move around the camera and with the number 5 we can switch between the perspective and orthographic camera. Give it a try.
- When you click on the viewport (the zone where the model lives) you'll see how a circle changes position dynamically. This is called the cursor, and it controls where the next action will take place from.

There are modes that enable us to do different things to the model; we'll go over a few of them over the course of this chapter. The modes are at the bottom-left of the screen; they look like this:

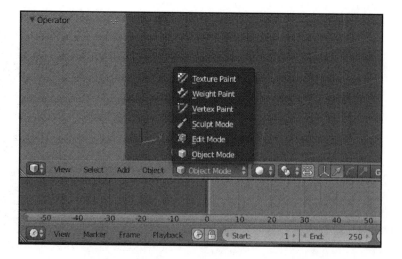

Let's take the Blender's default scene as a starting point. By default, Blender creates a cube, so we are going to start by modifying it to create the body of the gun.

To select an object, right click on the model (when **Object Mode** is active), and if you hold, the object moves along with the cursor.

The most basic tools you can use to start interacting with the objects in the scene are: move, rotate, and scale.

Move gizmo

The move gizmo is a handy tool to modify the model's position; it looks like this:

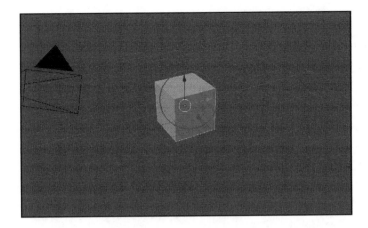

To move an object, press the *G* key and move the mouse. Or you can use the **Translate** tool and click on one axis at a time for more accuracy. If you click on the middle circle of the gizmo the object will move freely. You can select it at the bottom-middle of the interface:

Scale gizmo

The scale gizmo does what its name says, it scales the model. It looks like this:

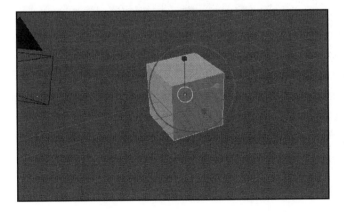

To scale, press the *S* key and move the mouse. Or you can use the **Scale** tool and click on one axis at a time for more accuracy. If you click on the middle circle of the gizmo the object will scale freely. You can select it at the bottom-middle of the interface:

Rotation gizmo

Again, as the name suggests, it rotates the model.

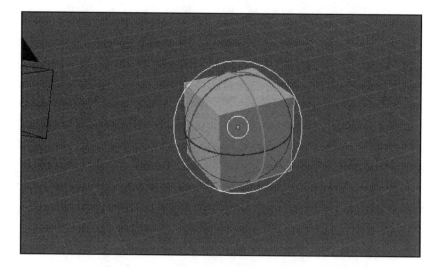

To rotate, press the *R* key and move the mouse. Or you can use the **Rotate** tool and click on one axis at a time for more accuracy. If you click on the middle circle of the gizmo the object will rotate freely. You can select it at the bottom-middle of the interface:

Sketching

In order to make our assets, we first need an idea of what we want and need for the game. Not only are sketches useful to give a better idea of how we want stuff to look, but you can also put this sketch inside Blender's background if you find this easier to follow the idea.

You can sketch in your drawing software of choice; we will choose by default **GraphicsGale** (`http://www.humanbalance.net/gale/us/download.html`). The freeware version is more than enough.

Again, we are only going to focus on the gun in this entire chapter so that you get a better idea about sketching.

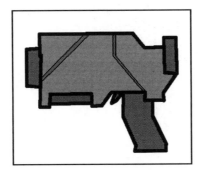

This is the model we made for the gun and it is a somewhat simple and alien stylized model. Now let us move on to the next step! The exciting part is coming!

 In order to get the assets with all its parts working correctly, you'll have to play around Blender a little bit and then export and import to your application. This process has been explained and simplified as much as possible to fit our needs, but you are recommended to try things out and get to know how the assets work within Blender and LibGDX. The importing process will be explained in `Chapter 5`, *Starting to Look Like an Actual Game*.

Game asset pipeline in Blender

We are going to explore the full process of a 3D asset: modeling, texturing, rigging, and animating our gun inside Blender. Run it and let's start right away!

Modeling

Finally, we can move on to the most exciting part of the chapter, modeling:

1. Select the **Scale** tool (explained in the basics).
2. Make the cube wider on the y and z axis by clicking on the corresponding axis on the gizmo (one axis at a time).
3. You can cancel any change on the model by right-clicking the mouse button or *Ctrl* + *Z* from the keyboard to undo, and *Ctrl* + *Shift* + *Z* to redo.

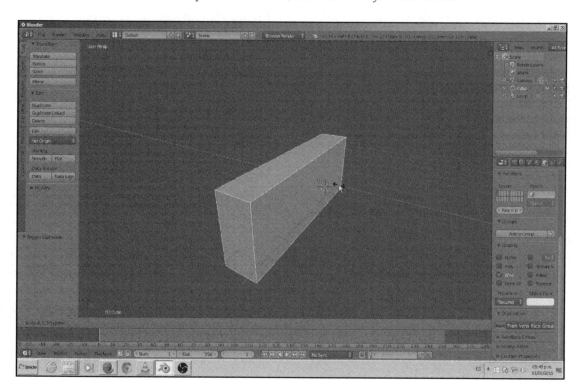

4. Duplicate the cube by pressing *Ctrl+C/ Ctrl+V* on **Object Mode** or *Shift+D* on both **Object Mode** and **Edit Mode**, then scale it down and move it below the first one. This will be our grip.

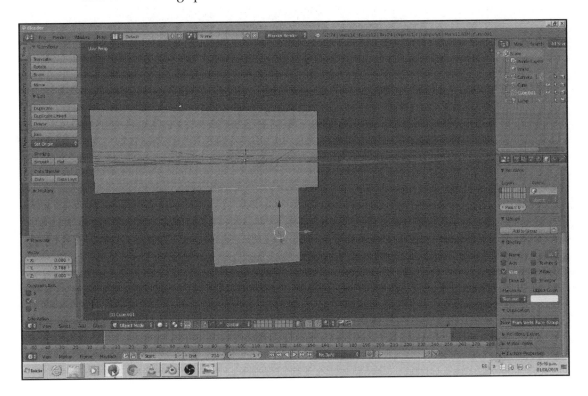

5. Now, just like we did with the body of the gun, scale the cube to make it thinner and taller.

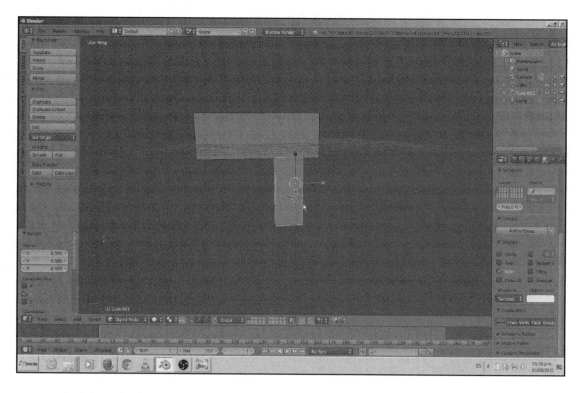

6. Select the first cube again (right-click over it).
7. Now, let's add some resolution by splitting the vertical edges in half using the **Loop Cut and Slice** tool. To get access to that tool we need to change the mode to **Edit Mode** from the bottom bar:

8. Now, by pressing *Ctrl+R*, we'll select **Loop Cut and Slice**. This will allow us to give the body of the gun a proper shape because of the addition of new vertices. The tool will show you a preview of how the cut will be made when you hover over an edge. You can use the mouse scroll wheel to increase or decrease the number of splits. Left-click to accept and right-click to abort.

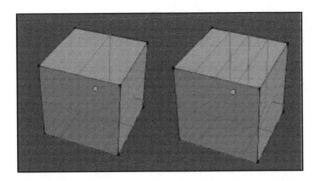

9. We will then modify individual components of the objects, as shown in the following screenshot:

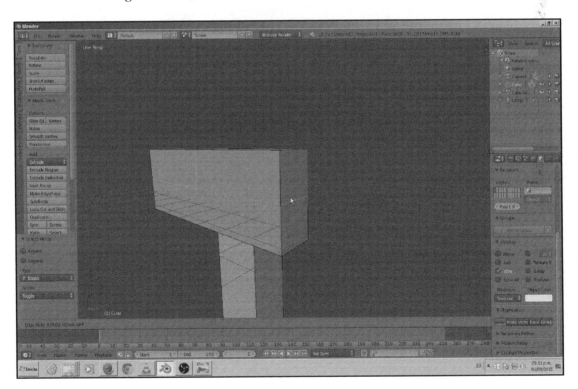

Before we move ahead, first let's take a look at some key concepts: Every polygonal object is made of faces, edges, and a set of vertices, which can be seen in the following screenshot:

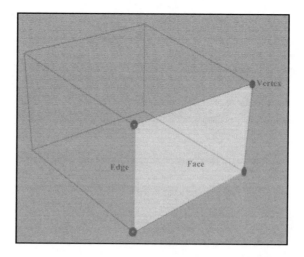

The following is an example in Blender:

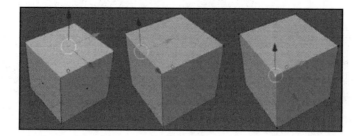

- **Vertex**: This is a point that holds positions in x,y, and z coordinates
- **Edge**: This is a connection between two vertices
- **Face**: This is a type of component formed by a set of closed edges

Now that we know about the different components, we can manipulate them individually or by groups in order to get a shape close to the original concept as much as possible.

The theory is simple; you start from a basic cube. You scale it to the proper size of your final object; this is known as the blocking stage. Once you have your blocking in place, you can begin to add more points in order to sculpt out the shape.

Now go to **Edit Mode**, make sure you are on **Face select** mode (select it from the bottom-middle), and then select the upper-back face by right-clicking over it.

Move it backwards. You can also manipulate the vertices of this face. You will see how the form starts to change; it won't be a simple cube anymore.

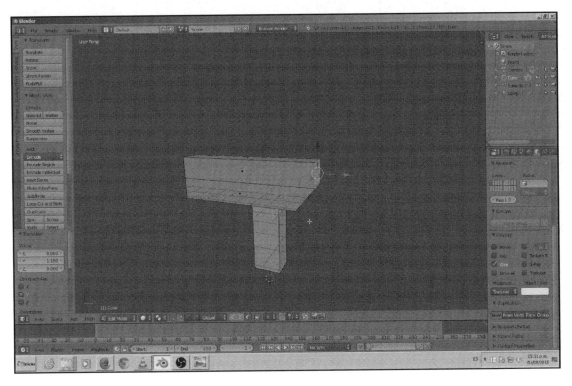

Split the horizontal edges by adding a loop vertically around the middle using the **Loop Cut** tool. This will split the faces in half, giving us more faces to work with. This is needed to add more shape to the gun body.

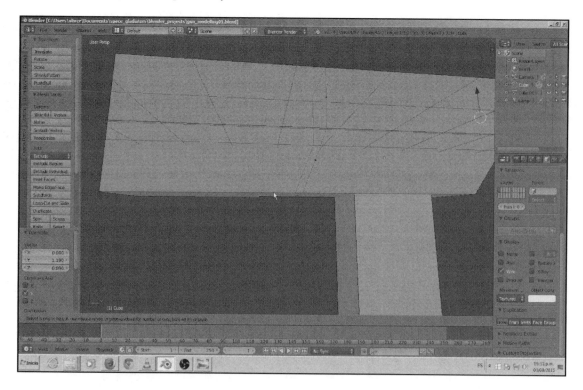

Execute an **Extrude** operation (*E* key or **Tool** bar on the left) on the bottom of the main cannon, making it look like a forend.

Execute another split operation on the middle of the back section, again vertically, so we can modify the shape of the top of the gun body. Don't worry if the new edges don't look straight. We are just interested in getting more faces at the top.

We can now select the **Scale** gizmo and try to get the edges as straight as possible.

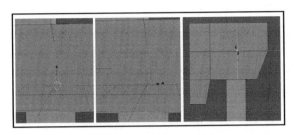

Extrude the upper faces of the gun body. The extrusion command pushes the faces and creates new faces to connect with the old ones leaving no gaps between.

 Faces that are selected will be shown in a yellow overlay color while the other ones will have a dot in the middle; this is the center of a face. Remember that you have to be in **Edit Mode** and switch the selection mode to **Faces select** in the bottom bar to the right of **Edit Mode**.

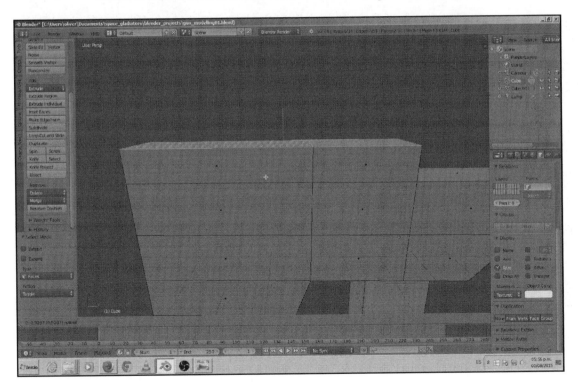

Go back to **Object Mode**, select our grip cube, switch to **Edit Mode**, and add an edge loop so we can begin shaping it.

So far we have a basic cube shape. Using the tools we mentioned before, add an edge loop above the middle, and cut the polygons horizontally. After that, move the lowest vertices back, to break up that basic cubic shape.

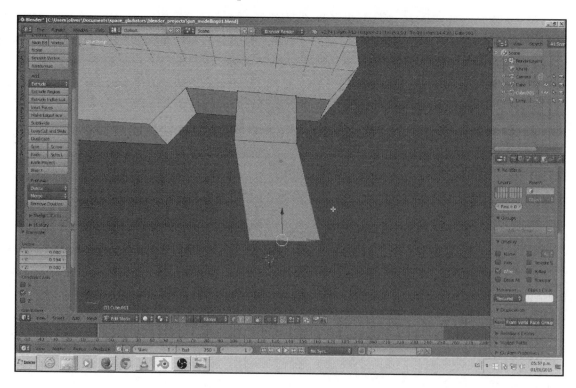

Extrude the bottom face downward.

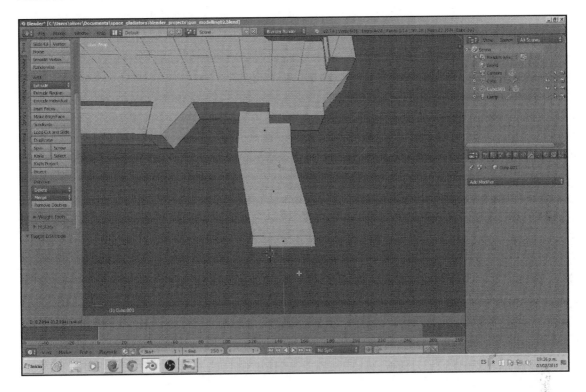

Go back to **Object Mode**, select our main mesh, switch to **Edit Mode**, and insert an edge loop in the middle of the geometry (vertically), again using the **Loop Cut** tool.

There is no need to double the work when you can use the **Mirror** tools that Blender provides; basically, you work on one side of the object while it mirrors the same changes on the other side. This is applicable for symmetrical objects too.

If you double-click, the loop will be placed in the exact center.

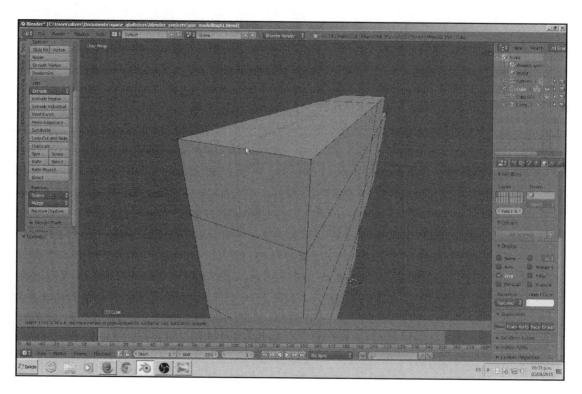

Select and delete half of the faces of the geometry by pressing the *Delete* key, and then choose **Faces** from the drop-down menu.

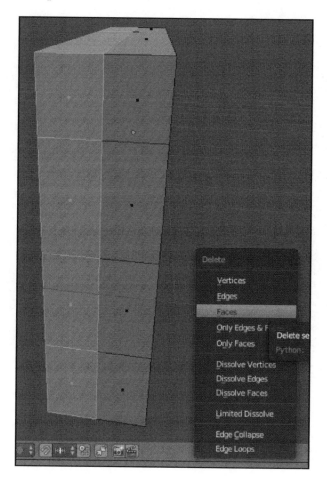

Now apply the **Mirror** modifier found in the **Add Modifier** list for the objects, on the left side under the outliner.

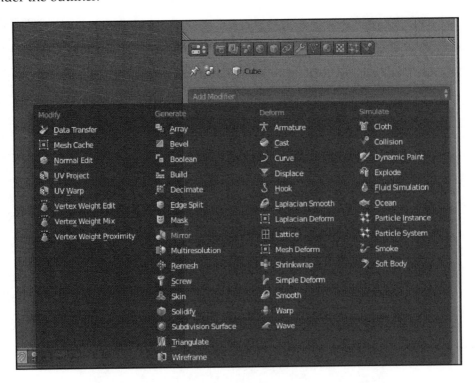

Take the **Knife** tool and let's cut some faces. This tool will allow us to cut edges by adding new points. Just click over an edge to create a point and then click over another edge. They will be connected automatically with edges, causing the faces to be split.

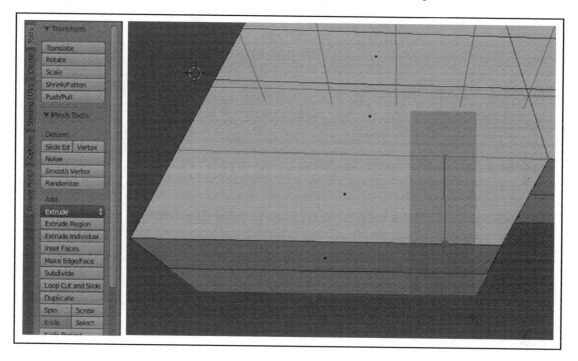

If the edges you just created don't look straight, you can always select the edges and scale them in. In this case, we are scaling the y axis. To do this, you need to select the **Scale** tool (*S* key), then press the key of the perpendicular axis you want to align, and then press (zero on the keyboard).

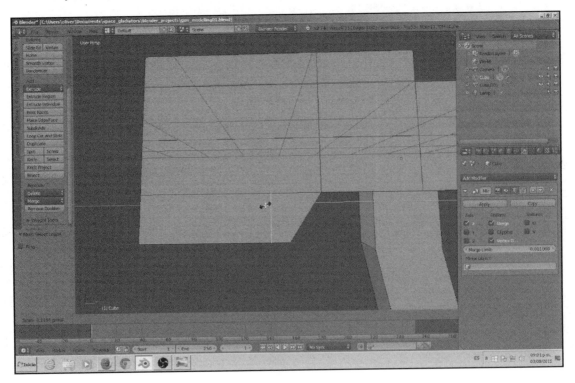

Cut the faces again as follows using the **Knife** tool, and scale the edges in if necessary:

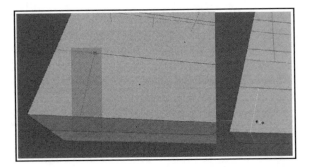

Extrude some faces as shown in the following screenshot after selecting them. This is to give the gun more detail and when you get to the texturing stage this will come in handy:

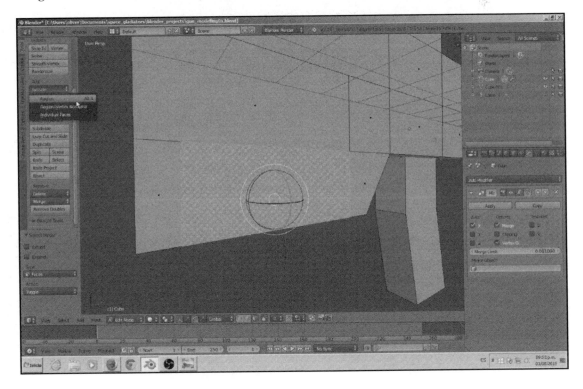

If some edges go too far, use the move tool to bring them back, as the extrude action is not always perfect. To do this, select the edges that go beyond the middle and move them to the center, so that they align with the rest.

While you are modeling, sometimes you may want to hide the mirrored side of the mesh to get rid of distractions; you can do so by going to the **Modifiers** list (under the **Outliner**), then clicking on the eye icon of the mirror you created last.

 As a side note, when we edit models we can hide the models we are not editing by pressing the / key in the number pad and pressing it once more to display them again.

Now move some faces back to make a shape similar to a forend.

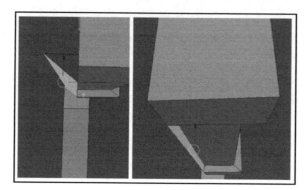

Go to **Face Select** mode and select and delete that extra face that was created after we extruded.

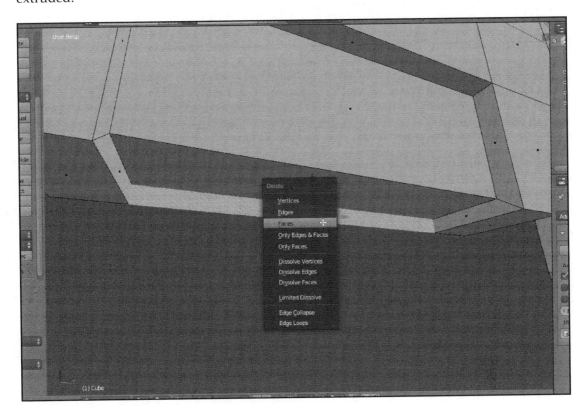

Now it should look like this; it should give a feeling of being a forend:

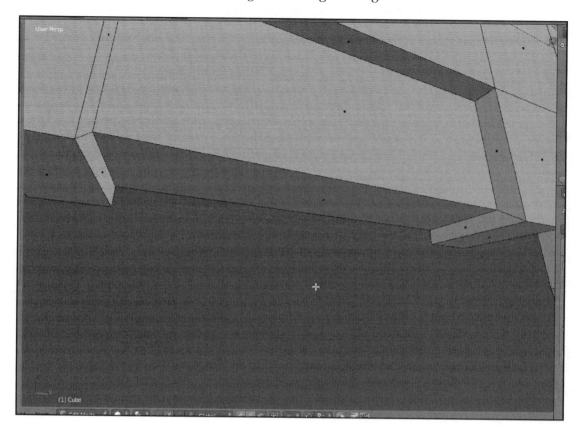

Cut and extrude some of the frontal faces of the gun body to make some room for the muzzle. Extrude and extract what's going to be our muzzle:

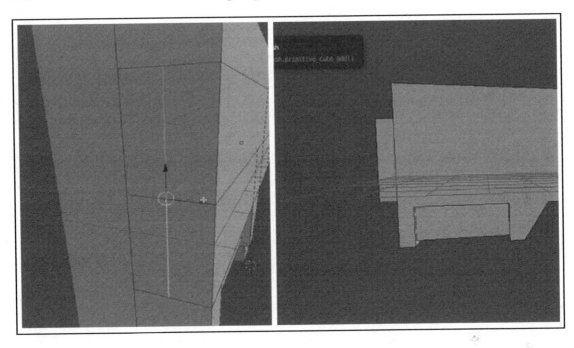

Now let's add some details on the back. Use the **Knife** tool again to cut some faces on the back. This will give us new faces. Extrude them up and align the edges that go too far with the Move tool.

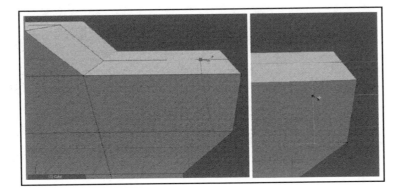

Apply an Inset to some faces (you can find this tool on the **Tool** palette) and then straighten the lines at the top or we'll have a sight with no use at that spot because of the form.

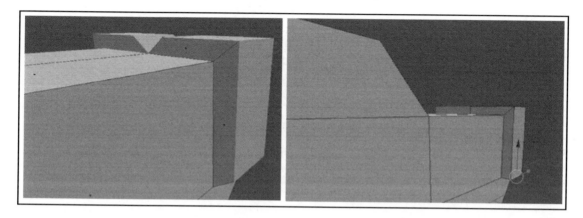

Next, pick the inside faces and extrude them inside. You'll have to work a little bit to make it look like ours; it takes a bit of practice. If you followed the steps this far you should have an idea of how, using the axis accessible from the keyboard (x, y, z).

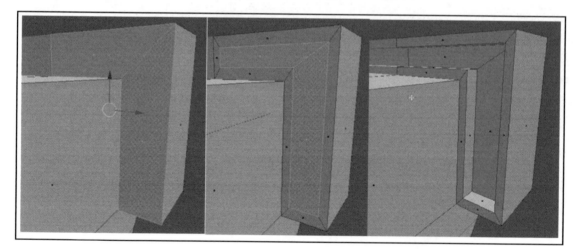

At this point, you already know most of the basics and you can keep doing a few more details or add the details you want. If we choose to follow our first sketch, the model should end up looking something like this:

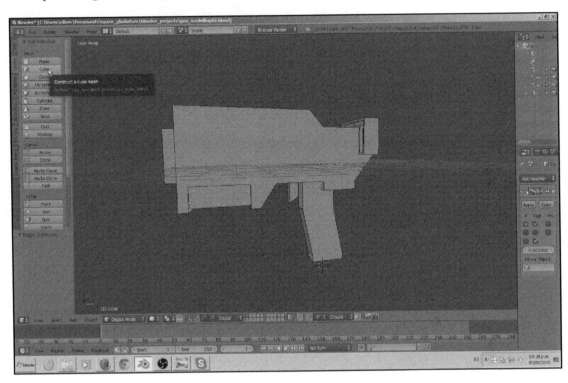

Once you are happy with the model, you can apply the **Mirror** modifier so the model will be one instead of two.

Save your model with *Ctrl + S* or **File | Save** and let's continue with texturing, but first we need a UV mapping for it.

UV mapping

In this section, we are going to take a look at the process of preparing the model for texturing.

UV mapping is the process that allows us to give 2D coordinates to a 3D model; that way each point knows what pixels they need to look at on a 2D texture. This process is vital when you want to texture your model using a photographic editing application, but if you are going to texture your model in a 3D application it is more flexible, because the UV mapping doesn't have to be perfect. In this case, we are going to paint directly in the 3D view and use the power of the painting brushes that Blender offers us.

Let's begin by setting up Blender's interface for texturing. First split the viewport in half by drawing the top-right corner of the perspective view, just above the plus icon. This will create a second view on the right side (you can always go back by drawing the corner to the default position).

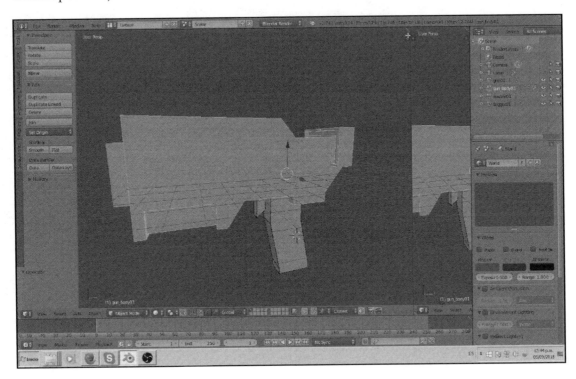

Switch the right view to **UV/Image Editor** by clicking on the icon located on the bottom-left side of the right view we just created.

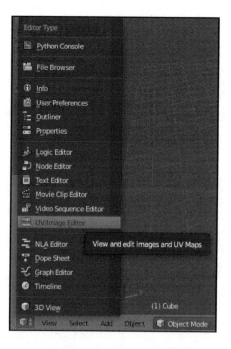

Change to **Edit Mode** in the left view and switch to the **Shading/UV** tab in the left toolbar. Here you will find the tools needed for making the UVs.

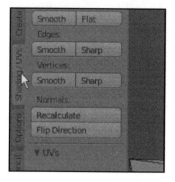

 After some work, we merged a few vertices and deleted some edges in order to make it look more like our first sketch.

If you want, you can start a range of edge selections where you want to cut the UVs. These are called seams, and they will let the UV map be separated by sections. They mark edges with colors. This is useful if you want to have a cleaner UV map, but it's not 100% necessary. We can mark seams on the bottom of the **Shading/UVs** tab.

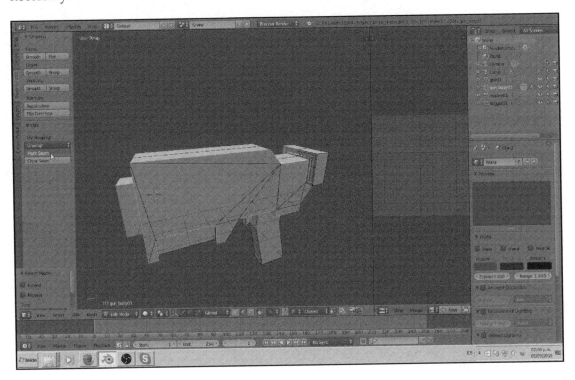

Select all the faces by pressing the *A* key on the keyboard and then hit the **Unwrap** button in the left toolbar (or *U* on the keyboard and select **Unwrap**). The UV result will most likely be different from what we have, but you can also try the option **Smart UV** and try between the two a few times, with different results, until you are satisfied.

Work on each object UV separately first, and once you have a UV you're satisfied with, join the objects by pressing *Ctrl + J* and click **Object**.

You can hide the objects from view by clicking on the eye of each in the outliner (top-right).

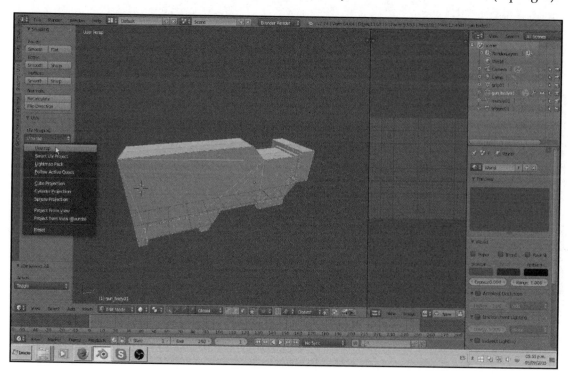

You'll see the unwrap result in the UV view (our right view):

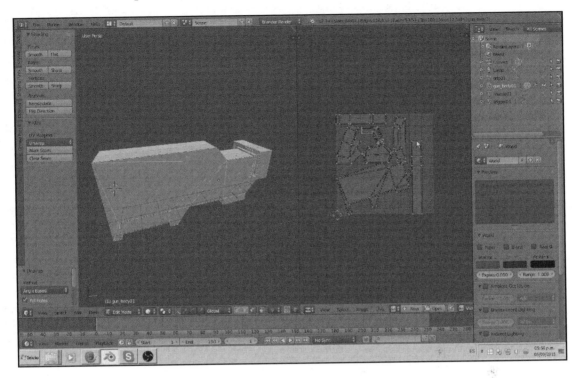

At this point, you can export the UV layout so you can have a reference to work with on an image editing application to texture the model, or you can texture it with Blender (more on this in the next section). Make sure to be in **Edit Mode** to access the **UVs** button in the toolbar at the bottom-right so you can export the UV. After you paint the texture in an image editor application, you can bring it back to Blender by clicking on **Image** | **Replace Image**, and picking your file from the prompt window.

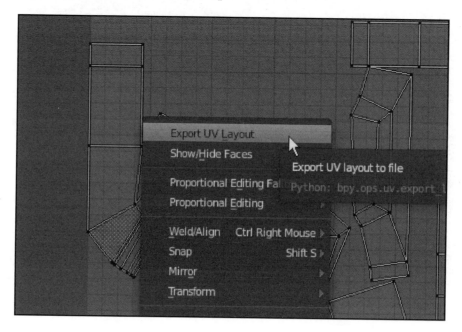

If necessary, move the individual UVs around so they don't overlay each other; you can do that by using the selection components (Points, Edges, Faces, and Islands; see bottom-left of the image). Just keep in mind that these UVs should always remain inside the square from 0-1 in U, and 0-1 in V coordinates.

Texturing

Now it's time to texture. In this section, we are going to take a look at Blender's texturing tool to create the texture of our gun (hand-painted style). Start by changing to **Texture Paint** mode under the bottom bar. Don't worry about having two separate screens, as we need them now.

1. On the **Tool** Palette (left tool bar) select **Add Paint Slot**, and from the drop-down menu select **Diffuse color**.

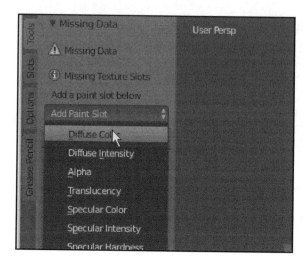

2. Set the resolution of your texture. In this case, we are going to use **1024 px** for **Width** and **1024 px** for **Height**. Click **OK**.

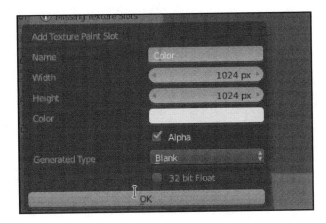

3. Change the right panel to **UV/Image Editor**.
4. On the **UV/Image Editor** select the image texture to be the diffuse map you just created.

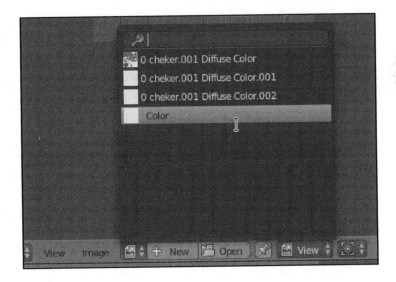

5. On the **UV/Image Editor** change the mode from **View** to **Paint**. This will allow you to paint directly onto the flat UVs.

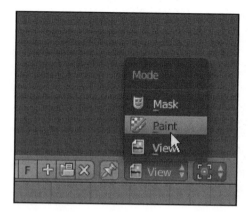

6. Pick a base color for the gun and start painting, either from the **3D View** or the **UV/Image Editor**.

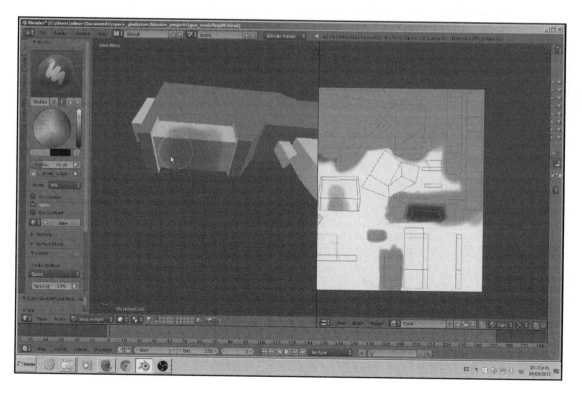

After spending more time working on the painting process, our gun starts to look like this. Once you get accustomed to the tools you'll find it easy:

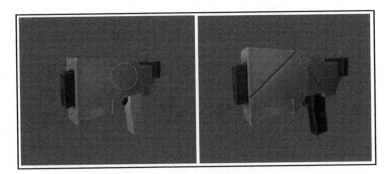

You should play around a bit and get to learn Blender's brushes and other tools for texturing. In general, you can get fast and good enough textures just by using those tools.

When you feel happy with the texture, click on the **Save As Image** button located in the **Image** menu (on the **UV/Image Editor** view). This will save your image in a standard file output, ready to be used in any other software.

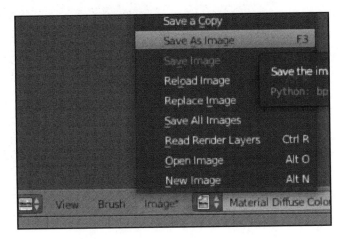

We now have to set this texture to our model and its material. This is needed for the model to render the texture into LibGDX. For this, we need to go to the right toolbar and click **Material**:

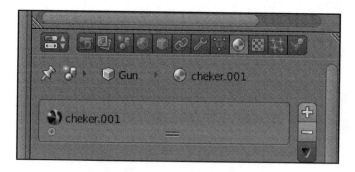

Check **Face Textures**:

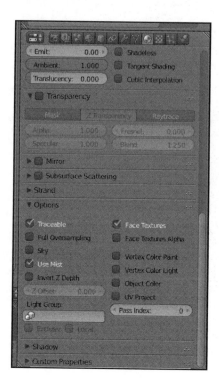

Then go to the **Texture** section and set up as **Image or Movie** and select the exported image you just made:

The only thing left now is to set the coordinates:

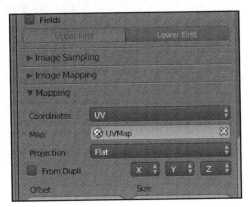

Bam! In order to see the texture in other modes, we change the Viewport Shading (the small button at the right of the modes at the bottom-left) to **Texture**.

First steps to animation – rigging

In this section, we are going to take a look at the process of setting up the controls to animate the gun.

There are different ways of creating 3D animations, but when dealing with animation for games it is important to build a bone structure inside the objects so that the game engine knows how the object moves in real life. These bones will drive the geometries that they'll be attached to, but the animator needs a way to move the bones without actually having to grab them directly. For this reason, we need to build control curves. These curves will contain the animation keyframes needed for the performance of the object movement.

First of all, select all the models and freeze their transformations. For this, we first need to go back to **Object Mode**; in the bottom toolbar select **Object | Apply | Location**.

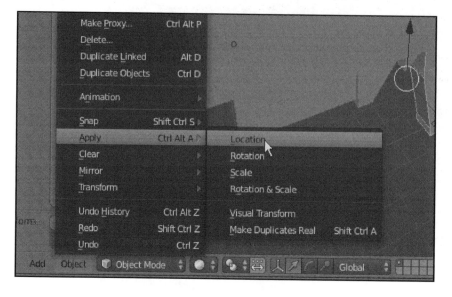

Select the gun body and hit the **Armature** button in the **Create** tab on the left tool bar. This will create a bone that we need for the animations.

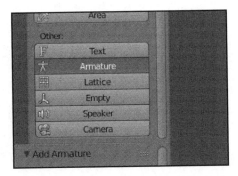

Toggle the quad view (*Ctrl* + *Alt* + *Q* or bottom bar **View** | **Toggle Quad View**), and change the **Viewport Shading** to **Wireframe** in the bottom bar.

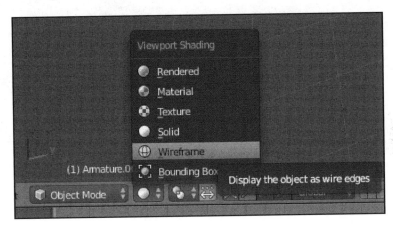

Now it is easier to position the bone and joints (which are the circles at the sides of the bone). Adjust its position and rotation if needed, so it's aligned inside the gun body. To adjust the position of joints you'll have to switch to **Edit Mode**, otherwise you will be moving the bone.

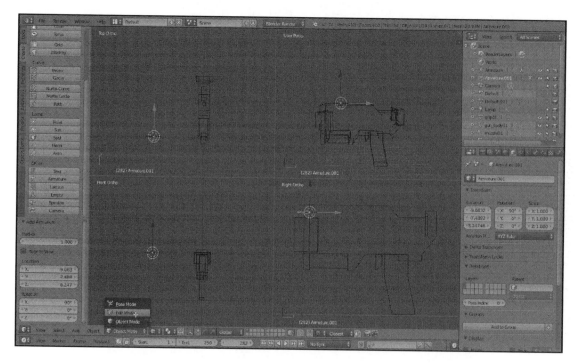

Place it at the back of the gun.

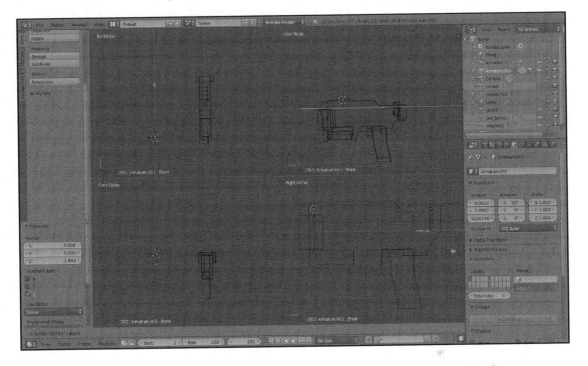

Once the bone is positioned and scaled and rotated if needed, we clone the bone through the joint by pressing *E* on the keyboard. Just select the joint you want to clone and press *E*. We are going to clone it two times in order to show the bone parenting and how it can move different parts of a 3D model.

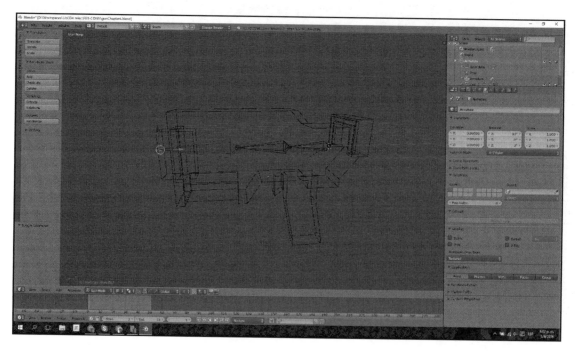

In **Object Mode**, first select the objects and then the bone, and parent them by going to **Object | Parent | With Automatic Weights** or press *Ctrl + P* | **With Automatic Weights**.

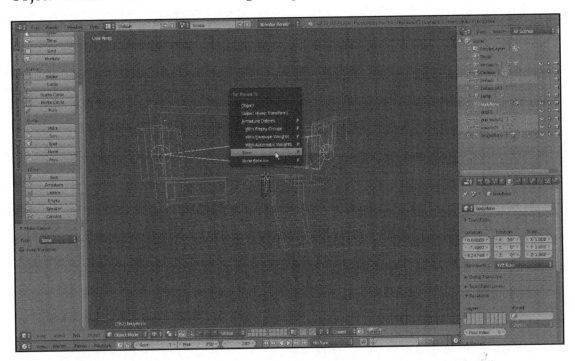

Now you have the bones parenting the gun, which means that moving one of them will cause the gun to do weird things!

That's all there is for rigging; we will now be moving on to animation.

Animation

Now we need to go to **Pose Mode** to adjust bone transformations. Open the **Transform** menu by clicking on the + icon located on the top-right:

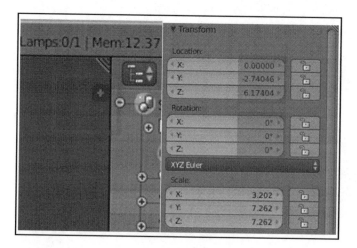

1. Open the **Dope Sheet** perspective.

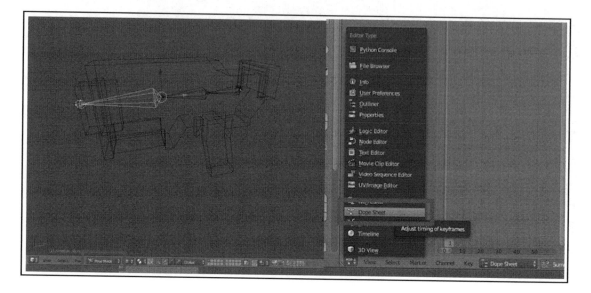

2. With **Pose Mode**, in the **Dope Sheet** perspective, we change it to **Action Editor** mode.

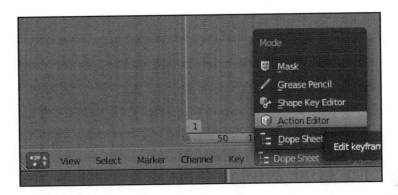

3. Now create a new action.

4. We want to give our animation a simple name to use inside the code. After pressing **New**, you'll see the space to add a name. We will name it shoot.

5. Now we can actually start animating. Pick the frame (zero) over the timeline bar (the bottom perspective) and then go over the model and press *I* on the keyboard.

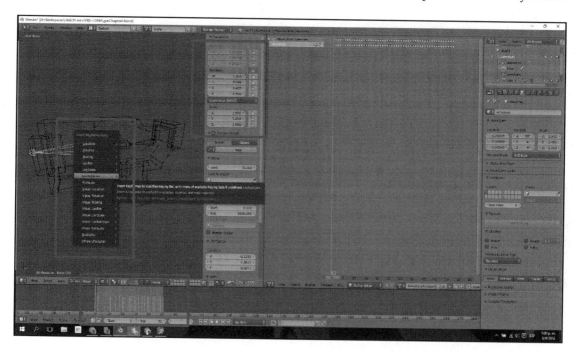

6. With the menu that opens up when you press *I* on the keyboard, you get to see different options. We choose to just use **Scaling** for our gun, but you can try your own keyframes.

7. Skip over a few frames, make the move you want to make with the bone (in our case, scaling), and save the keyframe.

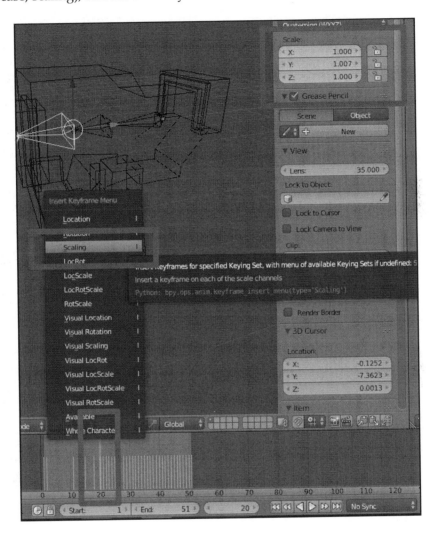

8. You don't have to save every frame of the maximum number of keyframes you want to fill. We will do this for start, middle animation, and finish.

9. Test the animation by clicking on the Play button in the middle of the Timeline perspective (bottom-right of the last image).

10. After you have saved all of your animation keyframes with the maximum number of frames you want to use, the only thing left is to export the model!

 You can have multiple animations by just clicking the + icon by the right of the name of the animation.

Exporting

Once you have finished the pipeline (model, UV, texture, rig, animate) for your specific asset, which can or cannot contain all the steps of the pipeline, it is time to export with the simple **File | Export | FBX**.

Now, there are a couple of things to bear in mind:

- Firstly, FBX is not a directly compatible file format for use in LibGDX, but we need to carry out an extra step with a tool from LibGDX that transforms it to files prepared for complex model rendering. These are G3DB and G3DJ. The first one is faster when loading and smaller, but is in binary. The other one is slower when loading but is in JSON format, which you can open up in any text reader. You should use G3DB for your release.

- Secondly, we can also export to OBJ (Wavefront) and import directly. But this approach is not suitable for complex models. Even the `ObjLoader` class included in LibGDX's API is only intended for testing and does not implement all the functionality you might want to use.

The steps for exporting are the same in both formats supported by Blender. We are going to export directly with FBX and will cover the transform to G3DB in the next chapter.

In the export window, only check **Armat** and **Mesh** from the **Export | FBX (.fbx)** option (you can select them by using the **Shift** key).

This process will export the geometry along with the animation and bones. The texture should be exported as we specified at the end of the texturing process.

Summary

We now have the tools and skills to create simple 3D assets for our game. This should help us take our game to the next level and also help us to see the bigger picture much better. We've learned how to set up Blender, how to create 3D assets from self-made sketches, and how to give them life using bones and animations. In the next chapter, we will finally import these into our game whilst tweening aspects of the game to improve it further.

Starting to Look Like an Actual Game

5

In this chapter, we will add our models with their animations and make them interact. We'll also add a space dome to start making it look like we are actually in space, and a modeled arena for which we will get the precise collision bounds.

In this chapter, we will cover the following topics:

- Adding models and animations
- Adding an additional camera for extra features
- Getting collision shape bounds from a static model
- Adding basic shadows

Models usable and ready to deploy with LibGDX

We can import models in a few types of file such as Wavefront (OBJ), as we explained in the *Exporting* section of Chapter 4, *Preparing Visuals*, which is a basic kind of file type that may or may not contain everything we need for the final deployment. Furthermore, OBJLoader class may not contain everything you'd want for a model loader either.

We want either FBX or OBJ, and we want to convert them to one of the two types that LibGDX handles best: G3DB and G3DJ.

For this, LibGDX provides a converter made by (Alias) Xoppa, called **Fbx-Conv**.

Downloading Fbx-Conv

Go to `https://libgdx.badlogicgames.com/tools.html` and download **Fbx-Conv** from
the **Download** hyperlink at the bottom of the app's box.

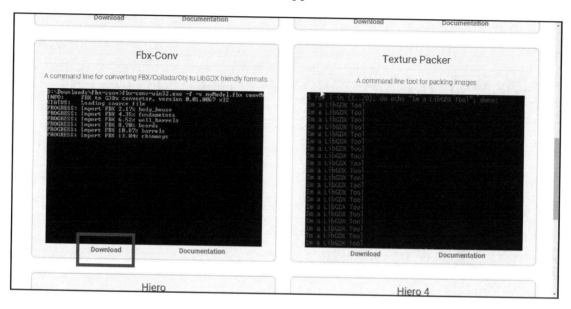

It will be a ZIP file, decompressed into a new and clean folder and easy to reach over the
command line.

Command-line usage

You can take a look at it in the following repository, `https://github.com/libgdx/fbx-con
v`:

```
Windows - fbx-conv-win32.exe [options] <input> [<output>]
Linux - fbx-conv-lin64 [options] <input> [<output>]
Mac - fbx-conv-mac [options] <input> [<output>]
```

Options/flags:

The following are the options, directly from the Fbx-Conv documentation (`https://github`
`.com/libgdx/fbx-conv`):

- `?`: This display helps information
- `<type>`: This sets the type of the output file to
- `f`: This flips the V texture coordinates
- `p`: This Packs vertex colors to one float
- `m <size>`: This shows the maximum amount of vertices or indices a mesh may contain (default: 32 k)
- `b <size>`: This shows the maximum amount of bones a nodepart can contain (default: 12)
- `w <size>`: This shows the maximum amount of bone weights per vertex (default: 4)
- `v`: Verbose prints additional progress information

Let's take a look at an example of these options:

```
fbx-conv-win32.exe -f -v myModel.fbx convertedModel.g3db
```

Adding our own gun model

There are a number of steps here for us to actually see our model being drawn and also animated. We'll go over them step by step. For this example, we'll use our gun model's file, which is in the FBX format.

Converting our gun model file

We will take our FBX file into the `fbx-conv` folder and convert it with the help of the following command:

```
D:\FBX-CONV>fbx-conv-[yourOS] -f -o G3DJ GUNMODEL.FBX
```

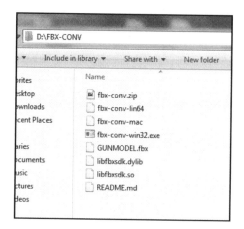

You should get to see something similar to what we have in the following image. We are using Windows, so we need to use `win32.exe`.

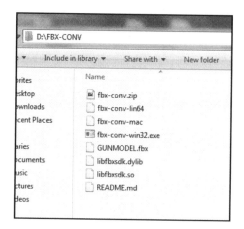

Let's go into a bit of detail here: we will now call our application, flip the V texture coordinates (-f), tell the app to convert it to the G3DJ file format (-o), and then give our file name. The default conversion is to the G3DB file format, and it's almost the same format as G3DJ but with a few differences. G3DB is faster to load but binary. G3DJ, on the other hand, is slower but has a JSON format that you can open and read. This can come in handy for a few things, for example, changing the material's opacity as seen in the following screenshot:

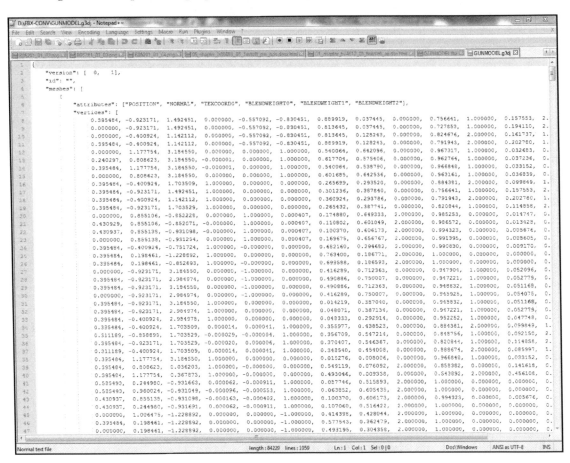

Importing the model, finally!

We can finally render the model after performing the following operations on it:

- Modeling
- Rigging
- Animating
- Giving the animation a name
- Getting the texture UV maps
- Texturing or painting (based on your preference and/or needs)
- Exporting
- Converting the file to a format

What we do here is, first, copy the converted file along with the texture file to our `assets` folder. For us, it is `Assets | Data` from our `Android` project:

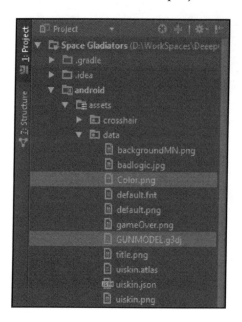

We'll then clean up and add the respective code to `GameWold.java`:

```
public class GameWorld {
    private static final boolean debug = false;
    private DebugDrawer debugDrawer;
    private Engine engine;
```

```
private Entity character, gun;
public BulletSystem bulletSystem;
public ModelBuilder modelBuilder = new ModelBuilder();
public PlayerSystem playerSystem;
private RenderSystem renderSystem;
Model wallHorizontal = modelBuilder.createBox(40, 20, 1,
        new Material(ColorAttribute.createDiffuse(Color.WHITE),
        ColorAttribute.createSpecular(Color.RED),
        FloatAttribute.createShininess(16f)),
        VertexAttributes.Usage.Position |
        VertexAttributes.Usage.Normal);
        Model wallVertical = modelBuilder.createBox(1, 20, 40,
        new Material(ColorAttribute.createDiffuse(Color.GREEN),
        ColorAttribute.createSpecular(Color.WHITE),
        FloatAttribute.createShininess(16f)),
        VertexAttributes.Usage.Position |
        VertexAttributes.Usage.Normal);
        Model groundModel = modelBuilder.createBox(40, 1, 40,
        new Material(ColorAttribute.createDiffuse(Color.YELLOW),
        ColorAttribute.createSpecular(Color.BLUE),FloatAttribute
        .createShininess(16f)), VertexAttributes.Usage.Position
        | VertexAttributes.Usage.Normal);
public GameWorld(GameUI gameUI) {
    Bullet.init();
    setDebug();
    addSystems(gameUI);
    addEntities();
}
private void setDebug() {
    if (debug) {
        debugDrawer = new DebugDrawer();
        debugDrawer.setDebugMode(btIDebugDraw.
        DebugDrawModes.DBG_MAX_DEBUG_DRAW_MODE);
    }
}
private void addEntities() {
    createGround();
    createPlayer(5, 3, 5);
    engine.addEntity(EntityFactory.createEnemy(bulletSystem, 5,
    3, 5));
}
private void createPlayer(float x, float y, float z) {
    character = EntityFactory.createPlayer(bulletSystem, x, y,
    z);
    engine.addEntity(character);
    engine.addEntity(gun = EntityFactory.loadGun(2.5f, -1.9f,
    -4));
    playerSystem.gun = gun;
```

```
        renderSystem.gun = gun;
    }

    private void createGround() {
        engine.addEntity(EntityFactory.
        createStaticEntity(groundModel, 0, 0, 0));
        engine.addEntity(EntityFactory.
        createStaticEntity(wallHorizontal, 0, 10, -20));
        engine.addEntity(EntityFactory.
        createStaticEntity(wallHorizontal, 0, 10, 20));
        engine.addEntity(EntityFactory.
        createStaticEntity(wallVertical, 20, 10, 0));
        engine.addEntity(EntityFactory.
        createStaticEntity(wallVertical, -20, 10, 0));
    }
    private void addSystems(GameUI gameUI) {
        engine = new Engine();
        engine.addSystem(renderSystem = new RenderSystem());
        engine.addSystem(bulletSystem = new BulletSystem());
        engine.addSystem(playerSystem = new PlayerSystem(this,
        gameUI, renderSystem.perspectiveCamera));
        engine.addSystem(new EnemySystem(this));
        engine.addSystem(new StatusSystem(this));
        if (debug) bulletSystem.collisionWorld.
        setDebugDrawer(this.debugDrawer);
    }
    public void render(float delta) {
        renderWorld(delta);
        checkPause();
    }
    private void checkPause() {
        ...
    }
    protected void renderWorld(float delta) {
        engine.update(delta);
        if (debug) {
            debugDrawer.begin(renderSystem.perspectiveCamera);
            bulletSystem.collisionWorld.debugDrawWorld();
            debugDrawer.end();
        }
    }
    public void resize(int width, int height) {
        renderSystem.resize(width, height);
    }
    public void dispose() {
        bulletSystem.collisionWorld.removeAction
        (character.getComponent(CharacterComponent.class)
        .characterController);
```

```
            bulletSystem.collisionWorld.removeCollisionObject
            (character.getComponent(CharacterComponent.class)
            .ghostObject);
            bulletSystem.dispose();
            bulletSystem = null;
            renderSystem.dispose();
            wallHorizontal.dispose();
            wallVertical.dispose();
            groundModel.dispose();
            character.getComponent(CharacterComponent.class)
            .characterController.dispose();
            character.getComponent(CharacterComponent.class)
            .ghostObject.dispose();
    character.getComponent(CharacterComponent.class).ghostShape.dispose();
        }
        public void remove(Entity entity) {
            engine.removeEntity(entity);
            bulletSystem.removeBody(entity);
        }
    }
```

We take the time to clean up our class and move all of the render calls into the
`RenderSystem.java`. So, this is our new `GameWorld` with no render classes other than the
`RenderSystem` instance and the new call to the `BulletSystem` class' render debug draw.
We'll add the gun as a new entity to the engine, and also keep the instance link to pass it to
the `Player` and the `RenderSystem` class. This last step is because we need to render the
gun with a different camera; we'll talk about this a little later. Most of the rest stays the
same.

We will also add the debug methods and classes here, such as the `SetDebug()` method,
debug Boolean, setting the debug drawer, and so on.

 The position we will pass to the gun constructor is the one that works for
us based on how big our gun is. Yours doesn't have to be the same, so play
around with it a bit by drawing it with the regular `PerspectiveCamera`
that you use for the models or use our gun model file of our game:

Next, fire up the `EntityFactory` class and create a new method called `loadGun(...)`:

```
public static Entity loadGun(float x, float y, float z) {
    ModelLoader<?> modelLoader = new G3dModelLoader(new
    JsonReader());
    ModelData modelData =
    modelLoader.loadModelData(Gdx.files.internal
    ("data/GUNMODEL.g3dj"));
    Model model = new Model(modelData, new
```

```
TextureProvider.FileTextureProvider());
ModelComponent modelComponent = new ModelComponent(model, x, y,
z);
modelComponent.instance.transform.rotate(0, 1, 0, 180);
Entity gunEntity = new Entity();
gunEntity.add(modelComponent);
gunEntity.add(new GunComponent());
gunEntity.add(new AnimationComponent(modelComponent.instance));
return gunEntity;
```

As usual, we will load our model, but with slightly different classes because of being a
G3DJ format. We will add a new component called GunComponent that we will use to filter
the render calls, and the AnimationComponent class to handle animation classes

Create an empty class called GunComponent.java:

```
public class GunComponent extends Component {
}
```

Next, we'll need a new component called AnimationComponent.java, so let's do that
now:

```
public class AnimationComponent extends Component {
    private AnimationController animationController;
    public AnimationComponent(ModelInstance instance) {
        animationController = new AnimationController(instance);
        animationController.allowSameAnimation = true;
    }
    public void animate(final String id, final int loops, final int
    speed) {
        animationController.animate(id, loops, speed, null, 0);
    }
    public void update(float delta) {
        animationController.update(delta);
    }
```

This is pretty straightforward; we need an AnimationController class to actually set the
animation we want to play. We set ModelInstance in the constructor and set
allowSameAnimation to true. If we don't do this, our animation will be called once if we
are repeating it. For our needs, this is enough for now.

We need one method where we set the ID of the animation (which we set over in Blender), the amount of loops, and the speed of it. We'll use this inside `PlayerSystem.java`:

```java
public class PlayerSystem extends EntitySystem implements EntityListener {
    public Entity gun;
...
    private void fire() {
    ...
        gun.getComponent(AnimationComponent.class)
        .animate("Armature|shoot" , 1, 3);
    }
```

We'll add the public global variable `Entity gun` and at the bottom of the `fire()` method, we will get the component (`AnimationComponent`) we call the `animate (...)` method and throw it the animation ID, the amount of loops, and the speed:

```java
public class RenderSystem extends EntitySystem {
    ...
    private static final float FOV = 67F;
    public PerspectiveCamera perspectiveCamera, gunCamera;
    public Entity gun;
    public RenderSystem() {
        perspectiveCamera = new PerspectiveCamera(FOV,
        Core.VIRTUAL_WIDTH, Core.VIRTUAL_HEIGHT);
        perspectiveCamera.far = 10000f;
        environment = new Environment();
        environment.set(new
        ColorAttribute(ColorAttribute.AmbientLight,
        0.5f, 0.5f, 0.5f, 1f));
        batch = new ModelBatch();
        gunCamera = new PerspectiveCamera
        (FOV, Core.VIRTUAL_WIDTH, Core.VIRTUAL_HEIGHT);
        gunCamera.far = 100f;
    }

    public void update(float delta) {
        drawModels();
    }
    private void drawModels() {
        batch.begin(perspectiveCamera);
        for (int i = 0; i < entities.size(); i++) {
            if (entities.get(i).getComponent(GunComponent.class) ==
            null) {
                ModelComponent mod =
                entities.get(i).getComponent(ModelComponent.class);
                batch.render(mod.instance, environment);
            }
        }
```

```
            batch.end();
            drawGun();
        }
    private void drawGun() {
            Gdx.gl.glClear(GL20.GL_DEPTH_BUFFER_BIT);
            batch.begin(gunCamera);
            batch.render(gun.getComponent(ModelComponent.class)
            .instance);
            gun.getComponent(AnimationComponent.class).update(delta);
            batch.end();
        }

    public void resize(int width, int height) {
            perspectiveCamera.viewportHeight = height;
            perspectiveCamera.viewportWidth = width;
            gunCamera.viewportHeight = height;
            gunCamera.viewportWidth = width;
        }
    public void dispose() {
            batch.dispose();
            batch = null;
        }
    }
```

As we said earlier, we have moved all of the render classes inside RenderSystem. We will add the global variables of the camera, add another PerspectiveCamera called GUNCAMERA, add the gun entity, and the static field of view (FOV) float variable.

Next, in the constructor, we will remove the parameters, clean up the method, and move all of the rendering code inside it. We will also construct the gunCamera variable at the bottom of the method.

In update (), we'll move all of the code inside a new method called drawModels() that will do all of the batch begin and end. And, at the end of this method, we'll call a new method called drawGun(). In this new method, we'll see a weird line at first that will clear the depth buffer; this is needed in order to display the gun with a different camera. Then, it has normal calls to ModelBatch in order to draw. And then, it gets AnimationComponent of the gun and updates it. This is needed for animations. Otherwise, they will not be played.

There's lots of different ways to display a gun in front of a player. We chose this one and it works for our game. Another way would be to place the model in front of the first camera that we use for the scene as well, but this takes a greater amount of work and we won't benefit from the extra work. Modern games may have it on the first camera so for example it can collide with objects.

And that's it! Run it and you should see something like this:

If you shoot (just click), the gun will play the animation we set in Blender.

Adding our own static arena

To continue our development, we need to now replace the arena we have as a playground for a nice and fitting model in regards to our game idea. We'll go onto the very basic of an important feature: collision shape.

Creating our model

We created a 3D arena with just primitive shapes and a couple of free images that are 2048×2048 from `http://www.textures.com/`. But a simple google search for `free 3D textures` should do:

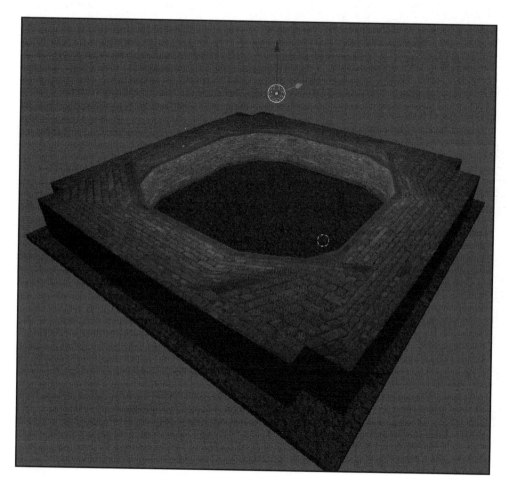

For a fast and perfect collision shape for a static model, we can use a handy static method provided by LibGDX. For our environment in Blender, for the types we used, we then need to export to OBJ to get the collision shape. So, let's start by exporting the model by navigating to **Export | WaveFront (.obj)**:

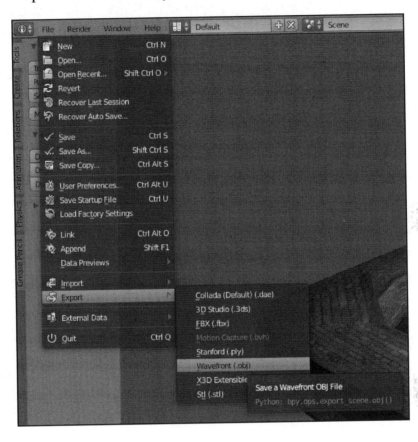

It's pretty straightforward; export to OBJ format and leave everything as it is (unless you are using a different version of Blender 2.74a).

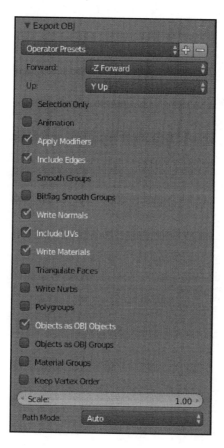

Next, we will convert to G3DJ with Fbx-Conv and just copy the files inside our `Assets` folder of the project. Keep in mind that you will need to copy the model file and the images you used in them.

Importing to our game and getting the collision bounds

After exporting from Blender and converting with Fbx-Conv, we now want to implement it.

We will need to modify the collision bounds because it's slightly different from our prototype one. For this, we can recalculate with the same classes. However, for that we'll also need to separate every part of our model. We want a fast solution for now, So, we will get a static collision bound from all the models together, which is the reason to first export OBJ from Blender.

Let's fire up the `GameWorld` class and change these two methods:

```
private void addEntities() {
    loadLevel();
    createPlayer(0, 6, 0);
}

private void loadLevel() {
    engine.addEntity(EntityFactory.loadScene(0, 0, 0));
}
```

As you may think, we will not use `createGround()` anymore, so feel free to remove it and the models and model builders. We will now have a cool model! Let's create a new method called `loadLevel()` in `GameWorld`, and make it add a new entity from a static method called `loadScene()` from `EntityFactory`:

```
public static Entity loadScene(int x, int y, int z) {
    Entity entity = new Entity();
    ModelLoader<?> modelLoader = new G3dModelLoader(new
    JsonReader());
    ModelData modelData =
    modelLoader.loadModelData(Gdx.files.internal
    ("data/arena.g3dj"));
    Model model = new Model(modelData, new
    TextureProvider.FileTextureProvider());
    ModelComponent modelComponent = new ModelComponent(model, x, y,
    z);
    entity.add(modelComponent);
    BulletComponent bulletComponent = new BulletComponent();
    btCollisionShape shape =
    Bullet.obtainStaticNodeShape(model.nodes);
    bulletComponent.bodyInfo = new
    btRigidBody.btRigidBodyConstructionInfo(0, null, shape,
    Vector3.Zero);
    bulletComponent.body = new
```

```
        btRigidBody(bulletComponent.bodyInfo);
        bulletComponent.body.userData = entity;
        bulletComponent.motionState = new
        MotionState(modelComponent.instance.transform);
        ((btRigidBody)  bulletComponent.body).setMotionState
        (bulletComponent.motionState);
        entity.add(bulletComponent);
        return entity;
    }
```

Built from `createStaticEntity()` with the difference of instead of using a `btBoxShape`, we will obtain the shape from a static method, `obtainStaticNodeShape(...)`. This method will give us exactly what it says, a static node shape.

Now, change the `debug` Boolean type in the `GameWorld`:

```
    public class GameWorld {
        private static final boolean debug = true;
        ...
    }
```

Let's run the file and take a look at the output:

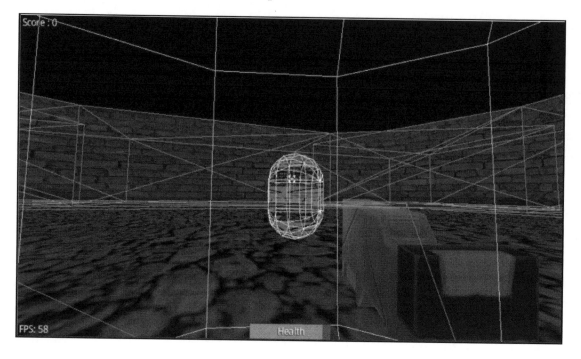

You will now see the collision bounds of all of our models except the gun, because we didn't set one for it, we don't need it. The collision bounds of the arena is pixel perfect, which is great, but this comes with a big downside—performance.

It's obvious that the application does more work to read it, so if you want the game to run smoothly on mobile devices, this may need lots of testing and improvements.

If you want to know more about collision bounds, you might want to check Bullet Physics Manual (`https://github.com/bulletphysics/bullet3/blob/master/docs/Bullet_User_Manual.pdf`), but for the basic idea, we have covered enough to get simple collision bounds.

To the next step! Enemies!

Enemy models!

It's time to work or fetch a model to represent our enemies. We have two options, model our own or get them from the Internet (either buy them or get them for free). We will show you how to work with a free model downloaded over the Internet.

Getting models from the Internet

With a simple Google search, you'll find a trillion sites to get 3D models from. They can come in different formats and sizes, with or without animations, and with one or more animations. We will get a model from `www.3drt.com`, and download the free alien test model from `http://3drt.com/store/free-downloads/free-monster-character.html`.

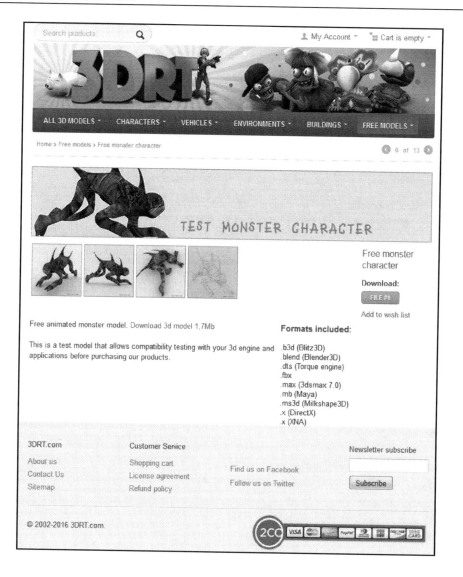

As you can see in the preceding image, the formats included are varied. We are mostly interested in FBX, but there's a variety of formats that Blender can import in case Fbx-Conv doesn't read it, so we can then export to FBX.

This ZIP file contains an FBX, so we can convert it directly.

Let's convert and then change `createEnemy(...)` from `EntityFactory.java`:

```java
public static Entity createEnemy(BulletSystem bulletSystem, float x, float
y, float z) {
    Entity entity = new Entity();
    ModelLoader<?> modelLoader = new G3dModelLoader(new
    JsonReader());
    ModelData modelData =
    modelLoader.loadModelData(Gdx.files.internal
    ("data/monster.g3dj"));
    if (enemyModel == null) {
        enemyModel = new Model(modelData, new
        TextureProvider.FileTextureProvider());
        for (Node node : enemyModel.nodes) node.scale.scl(0.0025f);
        enemyModel.calculateTransforms();
    }
    ModelComponent modelComponent = new ModelComponent(enemyModel,
    x, y, z);
    entity.add(modelComponent);
    CharacterComponent characterComponent = new
    CharacterComponent();
    characterComponent.ghostObject = new btPairCachingGhostObject();
    characterComponent.ghostObject.setWorldTransform
    (modelComponent.instance.transform);
    characterComponent.ghostShape = new btCapsuleShape(2f, 2f);
    characterComponent.ghostObject.setCollisionShape
    (characterComponent.ghostShape);
    characterComponent.ghostObject.setCollisionFlags
    (btCollisionObject.CollisionFlags.CF_CHARACTER_OBJECT);
    characterComponent.characterController = new
    btKinematicCharacterController
    (characterComponent.ghostObject, characterComponent.ghostShape,
    .35f);
    characterComponent.ghostObject.userData = entity;
    entity.add(characterComponent);
    bulletSystem.collisionWorld.addCollisionObject
    (entity.getComponent(CharacterComponent.class).ghostObject,
    (short)
    btBroadphaseProxy.CollisionFilterGroups.CharacterFilter,
    (short)
    (btBroadphaseProxy.CollisionFilterGroups.AllFilter));
bulletSystem.collisionWorld.addAction(entity.getComponent(CharacterComponen
t.class).characterController);
    entity.add(new EnemyComponent(EnemyComponent.STATE.HUNTING));
    entity.add(new StatusComponent());
    return entity;
}
```

Everything is normal, until we see the for loop that scales the nodes of the model (this is because we know that the model is much bigger than we need it to be) and then calculates the transforms.

At this point, the model is replaced and being drawn, badly, but still. Let's fix one thing at a time.

Preparing for more than one animation

When preparing our system for animations, first, we will need to open the G3DJ converted file to check the animation ID and keyframes. While it's not the best software for that, we can do this over IntelliJ.

If you press *Ctrl + F (cmd + F* for Mac OS X), it will open the search keyword in IntelliJ.

As you can see, the animation ID is `MilkShape3D Skele|DefaultAction` and it contains all animations in one place. You can also figure this out by just playing the animation.

What we need to do next is split this animation's keyframes to tell the `AnimationController` class where to start the animation and where to finish. For this, there's a number of ways to do it; we chose the programmer's way, which is to debug the app and check for the duration of the whole animation. We also have a TXT file that comes with the model and contains the keyframe numbers of animations called `animations-list.txt`.

First, let's open `AnimationComponent` class and add a new line:

```
public class AnimationComponent extends Component {
    ...
    public void animate(String id, float offset, float duration, int
    loopCount, int speed) {
        animationController.animate(id, offset, duration, loopCount,
        speed, null, 0);
    }
}
```

It's another `animate(...)` but it will have more parameters and call another animate method of `AnimationController`. This is to tell the controller exactly where to start playing the animation and where to stop it. The last parameters of the controller method are `AnimationListener` and transition time, which we don't need.

Next, let's set the duration of the animation:

```
21
22      public void animate(String id, float offset, float duration, int loopCount, int sp
23          animationController.animate(id, offset, duration, loopCount, speed, null, 0);
24      }
25
26      public void update(float delta) { animationController.update(delta); }
29      }
```

```
Variables
animationController = {AnimationController@1253}
    animationPool = {AnimationController$1@1254}
    current = {AnimationController$AnimationDesc@1255}
        listener = null
        animation = {Animation@1258}
            id = {String@1259} "Milkshape3D.Skele(DefaultAction"
            duration = 26.0
            nodeAnimations = {Array@1260} "[com.badlogic.gdx.graphics.g3d.model.NodeAnimation@6d7
```

After adding the model file to the `Assets` folder, we will open `AnimationComponent` and set a breakpoint in line **24** when closing the method we just added. Then, we will debug the app by pressing the top-right or *Shift + F9* button.

 To see line numbers in IntelliJ, you can go to **File** | **Settings** | **Editor** | **General** | **Appearance** | **Show Line Numbers**.

The app will stop right where our image is, and you can start opening the `AnimationController` instance in the **Variables** Tab: `AnimationComponent` | `current` | `animation` | `duration`. And there you go, 26.0. If you open `Animation.java` from the source, you'll see that it's a float.

Next, let's open the TXT file and start calculating how long those animations take in the float.

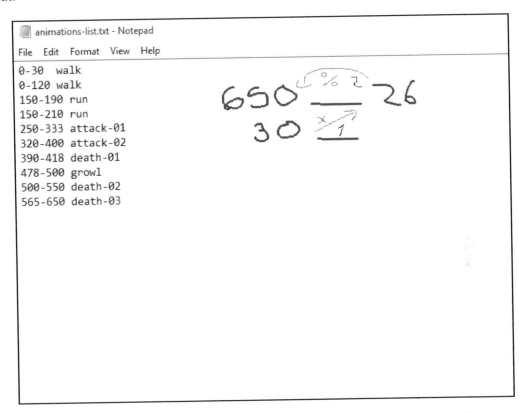

Let's break this down a bit more in detail. We know the duration of the full animation of the model is 26.0 float, the number of frames for all the animations is 650 frames. So if we want to know how long the first animation lasts we need to do with the *Rule of Three*:

- **N**: Number of frames we want to calculate how long they last in float
- **F**: Full duration of animation
- **FF**: Full number of Frames

So the first animation's duration can be calculated as *30 frames x 26 float % 650 frames = 1.2 float*.

Translated to Run-01: Offset = *150 x 26 / 650 = 6f.* Duration = *(190 x 26 / 650) – *OFFSET* = 1.6f.*

To save this data, let's create a new class called `EnemyAnimations.java`:

```
public class EnemyAnimations {
    public static final String id = "MilkShape3D
    Skele|DefaultAction";
    private final float duration = 26;
    public static final float offsetDeath2 = 22.6f;
    public static final float durationDeath2 = 3.4f;
    public static final float offsetRun1 = 6f;
    public static final float durationRun1 = 1.6f;
    public static final float offsetAttack1 = 10f;
    public static final float durationAttack1 = 3.32f;
}
```

Animation ID, full duration, durations, and offsets of a few of the animations that we want to use.

Keep in mind that you may have to do some extra calculation for the animations to be exact. The TXT file is not exact and we ended up with these numbers after some tests.

Run animation

For the run animation, we will just add a few lines to `createEnemy(...)`:

```
public static Entity createEnemy(BulletSystem bulletSystem, float x, float
y, float z) {
    ...
    entity.add(new EnemyComponent(EnemyComponent.STATE.HUNTING));
    AnimationComponent animationComponent = new
    AnimationComponent(modelComponent.instance);
    animationComponent.animate(EnemyAnimations.id,
    EnemyAnimations.offsetRun1,
    EnemyAnimations.durationRun1, -1, 1);
    entity.add(animationComponent);
    ...
}
```

Under the `EnemyComponent` addition, we will create an `AnimationComponent` instance and call the new `animate(...)` method with more parameters. And the `StatusComponent` class now takes the `AnimationComponent` instance.

Death animation and system

For the Death-02 animation, we will need a bit more. Now let's take a look at
`EntityFactory.java`:

```
public static Entity createEnemy(BulletSystem bulletSystem, float x, float
y, float z) {
    ...
    entity.add(new StatusComponent(animationComponent));
    ...
}
```

Next, add the `StatusComponent.java` file updates:

```
public class StatusComponent extends Component {
    private AnimationComponent animationComponent;
    public boolean alive, running, attacking;
    public float aliveStateTime;

    public StatusComponent(AnimationComponent animationComponent) {
        this.animationComponent = animationComponent;
        alive = true;
        running = true;
    }

    public void update(float delta) {
        if (!alive) aliveStateTime += delta;
    }

    public void setAlive(boolean alive) {
        this.alive = alive;
        playDeathAnim2();
    }

    private void playDeathAnim2() {
        animationComponent.animate(EnemyAnimations.id,
    EnemyAnimations.offsetDeath2, EnemyAnimations.durationDeath2, 1, 3);
    }
}
```

It will now receive the `AnimationComponent` instance in the constructor. It will need it for
playing animations.

We'll now update the status to gather the amount of time dead, until we make it disappear
and spawn another enemy. Another new method called `setAlive(...)`, and
`playDeathAnim2()`. The name of the latter method is because it's the second animation of
the model, the one that we are playing on death.

Let's update the `StatusSystem.java` updates:

```
public class StatusSystem extends EntitySystem {
    ...
    @Override
    public void update(float delta) {
        for (int i = 0; i < entities.size(); i++) {
            Entity entity = entities.get(i);
            entity.getComponent(StatusComponent.class).update(delta);
            if (entity.getComponent(StatusComponent.class)
            .aliveStateTime >= 3.4f) gameWorld.remove(entity);
        }
    }
}
```

There are some small changes to `update()`, where we changed the iterator, because it was creating an iterable object on every frame, changing to `for` block, updating the `StatusComponet`, and changing the `if` block to read the `aliveStateTime` variable. We want the entity to stay there a bit longer before it's removed.

Let's update the `PlayerSystem` class:

```
public class PlayerSystem extends EntitySystem implements EntityListener {
    ...
    private void fire() {
        ...
        if (rayTestCB.hasHit()) {
            ...
            if (((Entity)
            obj.userData).getComponent(EnemyComponent.class) !=
            null) {
                ((Entity)
                obj.userData).getComponent(StatusComponent.class)
                .setAlive(false);
                ...
            }
        }
        ...
    }
}
```

Just one more line, the one that sets the state of the enemy.

Last, but not the least, the `RenderSystem` class additions:

```
public class RenderSystem extends EntitySystem {
    private void drawModels(float delta) {
        ...
        for (int i = 0; i < entities.size(); i++) {
            if (entities.get(i).getComponent(GunComponent.class) ==
            null) {
                ...
                if (entities.get(i).getComponent
                (AnimationComponent.class) != null & Settings.Paused
                == false)
                entities.get(i).getComponent
                (AnimationComponent.class).update(delta);
            }
        }
        ...
    }
}
```

Nothing else is changed other than adding the animation update in `drawModels()`.

If you run it now, what will happen for this model in particular, is that it's alive but it's rotated. So, what we will do is open the Blender file contained in the ZIP file and modify the rotation:

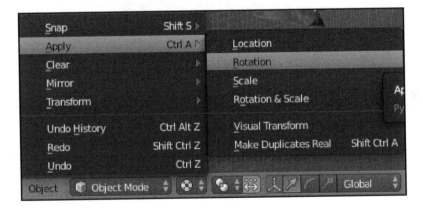

Open the Outliner and select the `MilkShape3D Skele` object. Then open the **Transform** panel, which is on the top-right (the plus sign) and modify the rotation **X** and Z to **90°**. Then move the model a bit lower in the Z axis by pressing G and then Z, move it almost to the middle of the model into the grid, and then click on **Object | Apply | Rotation**, and **Object | Apply | Location**.

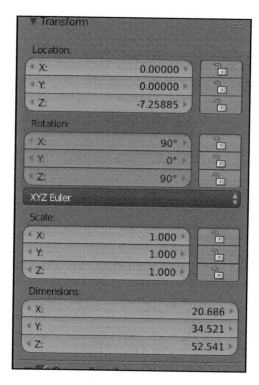

Then export the Armature and Mesh to FBX.

It's time to convert to G3DJ again and copy the files into the `Assets` folder.

Check it out.

Now look at that! The enemy is running and dying.

Improving the spawn function

With the arena and the enemy models in place, we should adjust our spawn method to give a less clunky feeling. We do this by cleaning our code and adjusting the spawn positions, pushing the enemies as far back on the top side of the arena as possible to make sure they don't just pop into existence in front of the player:

```
if (entities.size() < 1) spawnEnemy(getRandomSpawnIndex());
```

We replace the old spawn command in the first part of our `update()` method in the `EnemySystem` class with the preceding one-line statement. After this, we will create our new `spawnEnemy` function with an integer argument:

```
private void spawnEnemy(int randomSpawnIndex) {
    engine.addEntity(EntityFactory.createEnemy(gameWorld.bulletSystem,
xSpawns[randomSpawnIndex], 33, zSpawns[randomSpawnIndex]));
```

```
    }
```

This makes our code more readable as well as giving a more finished look to our game. While we are at it, we can also clean the class a bit.

Adding a SkyDome

If we want to be in space, we will need to give our players a bit of context. We may want to add something similar to a SkyDome that represents where we are.

Getting the model

As mentioned before, there's a number of different ways to get 3D models. We will take the one SkyDome that is in the LibGDX tests, but you can model your own if you want and add your own charm.

Or you can get it from our repository

(https://github.com/DeeepGames/SpaceGladiators/tree/Prototype/android/asset s).

Implementing

After pasting the files in the Assets folder, let's make the additions for the dome. Let's make the following changes to GameWorld.java:

```
public class GameWorld {
    ...
    private Entity dome;
    ...

    private void loadLevel() {
        ...
        engine.addEntity(dome = EntityFactory.loadDome(0, 0, 0));
        playerSystem.dome = dome;
    }
}
```

We will need a new global variable called dome. In loadLevel() method, add a new entity to the engine. At the same time, grab the entity instance. We will then pass that instance to PlayerSystem because we need the dome to follow the player, to be centered on the player, or else it will look weird.

Let's update the EntityFactory.java class:

```
public class EntityFactory {
    ...
    public static Entity loadDome(int x, int y, int z) {
        UBJsonReader jsonReader = new UBJsonReader();
        G3dModelLoader modelLoader = new G3dModelLoader(jsonReader);
        Model model =
        modelLoader.loadModel(Gdx.files.getFileHandle
        ("data/spacedome.g3db", Files.FileType.Internal));
        ModelComponent modelComponent = new ModelComponent(model, x,
        y, z);
        Entity entity = new Entity();
        entity.add(modelComponent);
        return entity;
    }
}
```

This is a regular entity load method, nothing fancy.

Now make the changes to the PlayerSystem.java class:

```
public class PlayerSystem extends EntitySystem implements EntityListener {
    ...
    public Entity dome;

    private void updateMovement(float delta) {
        ...
    dome.getComponent(ModelComponent.class)
    .instance.transform.setToTranslation(translation.x,
    translation.y, translation.z);

        if (Gdx.input.isKeyPressed(Input.Keys.SPACE))
            ...
    }
}
```

Just on top of the last if block, add the dome call and set the transform of the player. This way, the dome is centered where the player is.

Shadows and lights

It's now time to work on a bit of the environment. For this, there's also a number of ways to do it using either shaders or classes.

LibGDX uses a shader language that's called **GLSL**, capable of making amazing environments. We will not get into detail about this, but you can get more information from other Packt books, such as *OpenGL 4.0 Shading Language* (https://www.packtpub.com/game-development/opengl-4-shading-language-cookbook) and become an expert on it, making your games' ambiences a blast.

Adding a directional shadow with a light

We will go for the simple and fast solution that is using a debug class, DirectionalShadowLight.java, which is deprecated and should not be used, but for debug purposes and/or a simple game, it's enough.

So let's fire up RenderSystem.java:

```
public class RenderSystem extends EntitySystem {
    ...
    private DirectionalShadowLight shadowLight;

    public RenderSystem() {
        ...
        shadowLight = new DirectionalShadowLight(1024 * 5, 1024 * 5,
        200f, 200f, 1f, 300f);
        shadowLight.set(0.8f, 0.8f, 0.8f, 0, -0.1f, 0.1f);
        environment.add(shadowLight);
        environment.shadowMap = shadowLight;
        ...
    }

    public void update(float delta) {
        drawShadows(delta);
        ...
    }

    private void drawShadows(float delta) {
        shadowLight.begin(Vector3.Zero,
        perspectiveCamera.direction);
        batch.begin(shadowLight.getCamera());
        for (int x = 0; x < entities.size(); x++) {
            if (entities.get(x).getComponent(PlayerComponent.class)
            != null || entities.get(x).getComponent
```

```
                (EnemyComponent.class) != null) {
                    ModelComponent mod =
                    entities.get(x).getComponent(ModelComponent.class);
                    batch.render(mod.instance);
                }
                if (entities.get(x).getComponent
                    (AnimationComponent.class) != null & Settings.Paused
                    == false)
                    entities.get(x).getComponent
                    (AnimationComponent.class).update(delta);
            }
        batch.end();
        shadowLight.end();
    }

    private void drawModels() {
        batch.begin(perspectiveCamera);
        for (int i = 0; i < entities.size(); i++) {
            if (entities.get(i).getComponent(GunComponent.class) ==
            null) {
                ModelComponent mod = entities.get(i).getComponent
                (ModelComponent.class);
                batch.render(mod.instance, environment);
            }
        }
        batch.end();

        drawGun();
    }

    private void drawGun() {
        Gdx.gl.glClear(GL20.GL_DEPTH_BUFFER_BIT);
        batch.begin(gunCamera);
        batch.render(gun.getComponent
        (ModelComponent.class).instance);
        batch.end();
    }
}
```

We will start by adding the global variable and instantiating the shadowLight class with those values. These values are to make the light embrace more of the scene. Then, we set it for a color, add it to the environment, and the shadowMap variable of the environment instance.

Then we will create a new method called `drawShadows()`. It will do similar work to the `drawModels()`, but we will take the chance and make only one call to `AnimationComponents` of all the models that have it, removing the ones from `drawModels()` and `drawGun()`.

We can run and see it:

You can see the shadow at the side of the enemy and it also looks different.

Summary

In this chapter, you learned how to implement models from different sources, the use of animation and its classes, and making systems read those animations. Additionally, we also added shadows and a new camera to display the gun in front of the player. In the next chapter, we'll implement some audio in our game.

6
Spicing Up the Game

All games can use what is called **polishing** to make it look better; it's not only on the aesthetics but it can also improve the game design; for example, a fade away effect with particles can add immersion to what's happening in our game. Our mission with this chapter is, as mentioned before, to polish the look and feel of the game for the most part and other additions that can make a difference, such as performance. We'll go from a basic **particle system** to **UI tweening**, input on different platforms, exploring a bit of the .NET API that LibGDX brings, and a few more additions. We'll end up with a game that has more depth with only a few additions and learn a lot about continuous improvement.

In this chapter, we will cover the following topics:

- 3D particles and LibGDX's particle creator
- UI tweening
- .NET API and online leaderboards
- Platform recognition and input
- Frustum culling and performance
- Interfacing for different platforms
- Input on different platforms
- Testing on Android devices

3D particles and LibGDX 3D particle editor

We will use the built-in particle editor shipped with LibGDX, called **Flame**, to create our particle effects inside the game. It consists of a runnable Java file that can be downloaded from the official LibGDX tools page (`https://libgdx.badlogicgames.com/tools.html`). We'll walk you through a step-by-step process to make an "enemy-die" particle for your game; but, as you will discover, you can easily modify specific values for the particle to fit your specific needs.

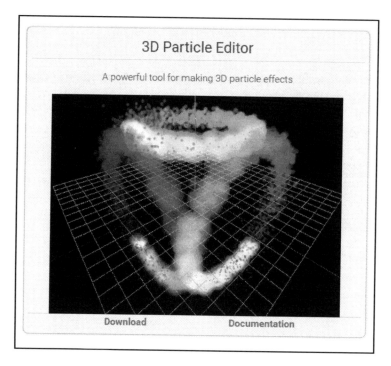

The UI contains three different sections; the viewport, the particle controller list, and the particle and editor properties. We'll focus solely on the properties aspect of the default particle.

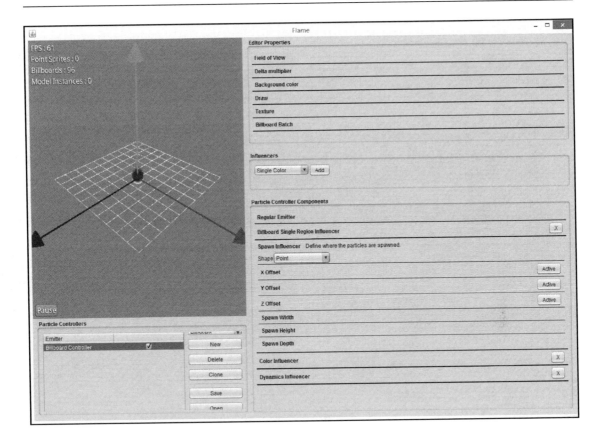

Particle effect types

There are three different kinds of 3D particle effect:

- **Billboards**: These are sprites that always face the camera (the `Decal` class in LibGDX is essentially a billboard).
- **PointSprites**: These draw a sprite to a single 3D point. They are simpler than billboards but more efficient.
- **ModelInstances**: These are instances of 3D models, but they're the most taxing type of particle effect in terms of performance.

We will now use **Billboard** particles, as shown in the following screenshot:

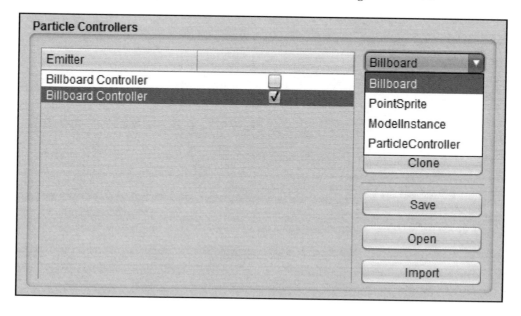

Emitter properties

We will just modify a field; we don't need more than one, but you can play with the app as it's very simple.

From the **Spawn Influencer**, we will pick a **Cylinder**. With this, we obtain what we want, which is somewhat similar to soda bubbles.

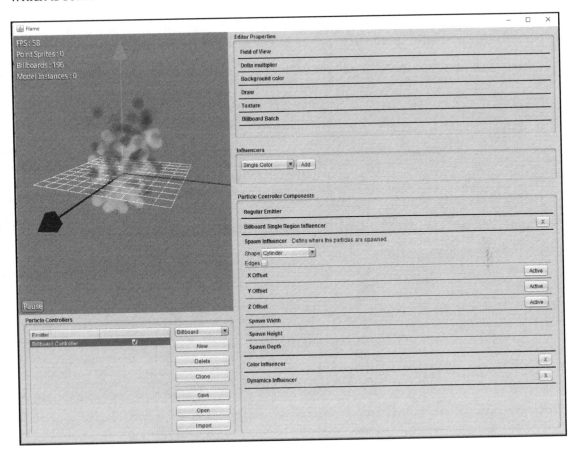

Saving and importing

Save, with the **Save** button, with the name you want and where you want, and add the prefix PFX later, when it's saved, then add it to your assets folder in the project.

We'll also need a texture that represents the rounded particle. For simplicity reasons, we will use a simple one that you can get from our asset folder (https://github.com/DeeepGames/SpaceGladiators) in the repository. The filename has to be pre-particle.png.

Adding the particle effect and a material attribute

Now it's time to work on the code. Not only will we add the particle we just created, but we will also add an attribute to the enemy's material to make it fade out. We'll start from the higher structure and go deeper.

First, open `GameWorld.java` and add the following:

```
private void addSystems(GameUI gameUI) {
    ...
    EntityFactory.renderSystem = renderSystem;
    ...
}
```

It's adding the `renderSystem` member to the `EntityFactory` class. We need to give it to the particle component.

Then, open the `EntityFactory.java` file, as shown in the following code:

```
public class EntityFactory {
    ...
    public static RenderSystem renderSystem;

    ...
    public static Entity createEnemy(BulletSystem bulletSystem,
    float x, float y, float z) {
        ...
        if (enemyModel == null) {
            ...

            Material material =
            enemyModelComponent.instance.materials.get(0);
            BlendingAttribute blendingAttribute;
            material.set(blendingAttribute = new
            BlendingAttribute(GL20.GL_SRC_ALPHA,
            GL20.GL_ONE_MINUS_SRC_ALPHA));
            enemyModelComponent.blendingAttribute =
            blendingAttribute;
        }
        ((BlendingAttribute)
        enemyModelComponent.instance.materials.get(0)
        .get(BlendingAttribute.Type)).opacity = 1;
        ...
        entity.add(new
        DieParticleComponent(renderSystem.particleSystem));
        return entity;
    }
```

```
}
```

This class adds a `RenderSystem` static field now. The `createEnemy` method now contains, separately, three new calls. It first gets the material from the `ModelInstance` class and adds `BlendingAttribute`, which also grabs its instance and sets it on the `ModelComponent` class. Second, it sets the `opacity` of the new `BlendingAttribute` instance to 1. And third, it adds a new component called `DieParticleComponent`, which receives the `RenderSystem` class' instance that it now contains a `ParticleSystem`.

We need to set the `opacity` field to 1 for every new creation of the enemy because we are reusing the last model instance created for it, and we want to make a fade-out effect on the model:

```
Now, ModelComponent.java:

public class ModelComponent extends Component {
    ...
    public BlendingAttribute blendingAttribute;

    ...
    public void update(float delta) {
        if (blendingAttribute != null)
            blendingAttribute.opacity = blendingAttribute.opacity -
            delta / 3;
    }
}
```

Add a global `BlendingAttribute` field and an `update` method that will reduce the `opacity` field when the enemy is not alive.

Now, let's create a new class called `DieParticleComponent` and add it to the `components` package:

```
public class DieParticleComponent extends Component {
    public ParticleEffect originalEffect;
    public boolean used = false;

    public DieParticleComponent(ParticleSystem particleSystem) {
        ParticleEffectLoader.ParticleEffectLoadParameter loadParam =
        new ParticleEffectLoader.ParticleEffectLoadParameter
        (particleSystem.getBatches());
        if (!Assets.assetManager.isLoaded("data/dieparticle.pfx")) {
            Assets.assetManager.load("data/dieparticle.pfx",
            ParticleEffect.class, loadParam);
```

```
            Assets.assetManager.finishLoading();
        }
        originalEffect =
        Assets.assetManager.get("data/dieparticle.pfx");
    }
}
```

Extend the `Component` class. On fields, it contains a `ParticleEffect` class member and a `boolean` variable. The constructor takes the `ParticleSystem` that is used to get the batches for `ParticleEffectLoader`. We will then check if a new `Assetmanager` in the `Assets` class hasn't loaded our particle yet and if not, it loads it and we tell it to take it's time for it. And finally, we will grab the instance of the loaded `ParticleEffect` class.

Going forward, open `Assets.java`:

```
public class Assets {
    ...
    public static AssetManager assetManager;

    public Assets() {
        ...
        assetManager = new AssetManager();
    }

    public static void dispose() {
        ...
        assetManager.dispose();
    }
}
```

It's as simple as that; we will now add `AssetManager` to it.

Next is `RenderSystem.java`:

```
public class RenderSystem extends EntitySystem {
    ...
    public static ParticleSystem particleSystem;

    public RenderSystem() {
        ...
        particleSystem = ParticleSystem.get();
        BillboardParticleBatch billboardParticleBatch = new
        BillboardParticleBatch();
        billboardParticleBatch.setCamera(perspectiveCamera);
        particleSystem.add(billboardParticleBatch);
    }
    ...
```

```
    private void drawModels() {
        ...
        renderParticleEffects();

        drawGun();
    }

    private void renderParticleEffects() {
        batch.begin(perspectiveCamera);
        particleSystem.update(); /* technically not necessary for
        rendering*/
        particleSystem.begin();
        particleSystem.draw();
        particleSystem.end();
        batch.render(particleSystem);
        batch.end();
    }
}
```

This does a bit more. It adds the `static` field of `ParticleSystem` and loads its instance on the constructor. Then, it loads the specific batch for the billboard particle (`BillboardParticleBatch`) and sets the camera to this batch too, and then adds to the particle system. In the `drawModels` method, we set a call for a new method called `renderParticleEffects` that contains standard draw calls.

Up next, and finally, is `EnemySystem.java` and its `update` method:

```
public void update(float delta) {
    ...
    for (int i = 0; i < entities.size(); i++) {
        ...
        ModelComponent playerModel =
        player.getComponent(ModelComponent.class);

        if (!e.getComponent(StatusComponent.class).alive)
            mod.update(delta);

        if (!e.getComponent(StatusComponent.class).alive &&
                !e.getComponent(DieParticleComponent.class).used) {
            e.getComponent(DieParticleComponent.class).used = true;
            ParticleEffect effect =
            e.getComponent(DieParticleComponent.class)
            .originalEffect.copy();
            ((RegularEmitter)
            effect.getControllers().first().emitter)
            .setEmissionMode
            (RegularEmitter.EmissionMode.EnabledUntilCycleEnd);
```

```
effect.setTransform(e.getComponent
(ModelComponent.class).instance.transform);
effect.scale(3.25f, 1, 1.5f);
effect.init();
effect.start();
RenderSystem.particleSystem.add(effect);
}
    ...
    }
}
```

After the call to get the player model, we will set an `if` call asking to see if the enemy is alive. If it's not, we will update the model component and it will start fading out the enemy model. Another `if` call asks if the enemy is alive and whether the particle is already used; this is last because it will play the same effect a bunch of times; so inside this `if` block, we'll set it to `true`. We will make a copy of the effect, set its emission mode to play once—for its live time (set in the particle editor by default to 3 seconds)—then set its transform to the same as the entity; then scale it a bit, initialize it, start it, and finally add it to the `ParticleSystem` class.

And that is it! Now our enemy should play a particle effect when we kill it and also fade out slowly.

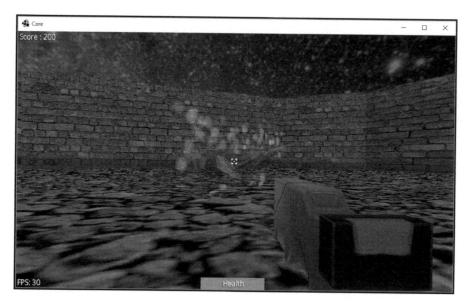

The effect is far from perfect but it gets the job done, and it works well on a mid-end Android phone. Test it on a mobile phone and see for yourself.

Mobile performance

At this point, we have the game working on the desktop; in general, it should work fine on most operating system and hardware as we are not using a lot of resources. But, we want to use LibGDX's capability to deploy on several platforms without much change.

Testing on Android

We prepared our project, from the start, to run on Android devices, but we never actually tested it on Android. If you run it on a mid-high end device now, it works really well after it loads the enemy model, of course.

The enemy model loads a new model every time it needs to spawn, so let's fix that.

Performance improvements on the enemy model

We now want to work a bit on performance. Though there's quite a lot of performance work we can do for our game, there's one big improvement we can do with the enemy model, and another small improvement that can be useful for bigger games, frustum culling.

```
Fire up EntityFactory:
public class EntityFactory {
    private static Model playerModel, enemyModel;
    private static Texture playerTexture;
    private static ModelBuilder modelBuilder;
    private static ModelData enemyModelData;
    private static ModelComponent enemyModelComponent;
    ...
    public static Entity createEnemy(BulletSystem bulletSystem,
        float x, float y, float z) {
        Entity entity = new Entity();
        ModelLoader<?> modelLoader = new G3dModelLoader(new
        JsonReader());
        if (enemyModel == null) {
            enemyModelData =
            modelLoader.loadModelData(Gdx.files.internal
            ("data/monster.g3dj"));
            enemyModel = new Model(enemyModelData, new
            TextureProvider.FileTextureProvider());
            for (Node node : enemyModel.nodes)
```

```
        node.scale.scl(0.0025f);
        enemyModel.calculateTransforms();
        enemyModelComponent = new ModelComponent(enemyModel, x,
        y, z);
    }
    enemyModelComponent.instance.transform.set
    (enemyModelComponent.matrix4.setTranslation(x, y, z));
    entity.add(enemyModelComponent);
    CharacterComponent characterComponent = new
    CharacterComponent();
    characterComponent.ghostObject = new
    btPairCachingGhostObject();
    characterComponent.ghostObject.setWorldTransform
    (enemyModelComponent.instance.transform);

    characterComponent.ghostShape = new btCapsuleShape(2f, 2f);
    characterComponent.ghostObject.setCollisionShape
    (characterComponent.ghostShape);
    characterComponent.ghostObject.setCollisionFlags
    (btCollisionObject.CollisionFlags.CF_CHARACTER_OBJECT);
    characterComponent.characterController = new
    btKinematicCharacterController
    (characterComponent.ghostObject,
    characterComponent.ghostShape, .35f);
    characterComponent.ghostObject.userData = entity;
    entity.add(characterComponent);
    bulletSystem.collisionWorld.addCollisionObject
    (entity.getComponent(CharacterComponent.class).ghostObject,
            (short)
    btBroadphaseProxy.CollisionFilterGroups.CharacterFilter,
            (short)
    (btBroadphaseProxy.CollisionFilterGroups.AllFilter));
    bulletSystem.collisionWorld.addAction
    (entity.getComponent(CharacterComponent.class)
    .characterController);
    entity.add(new
    EnemyComponent(EnemyComponent.STATE.HUNTING));
    AnimationComponent animationComponent = new
    AnimationComponent(enemyModelComponent.instance);
    animationComponent.animate(EnemyAnimations.id,
    EnemyAnimations.offsetRun1, EnemyAnimations.durationRun1,
    -1, 1);
    entity.add(animationComponent);
    entity.add(new StatusComponent(animationComponent));
    return entity;
    }
}
```

Only make changes to `createEnemy(...)`, what we can do is change a few class names and change `ModelData` and `ModelComponent` to global and static variables in order to not create objects again.

And that is it! Run the game again and it works really well as it is.

Performance improvements and frustum culling

For simplicity reasons, we will use this simple method to create shadows, and it's up you to improve and explore its options with the actual models.

Let's fire up the `RenderSystem` class and add this:

```
public class RenderSystem extends EntitySystem {
    ...

    private boolean isVisible(Camera cam, final ModelInstance
    instance) {
        return
        cam.frustum.pointInFrustum(instance.transform.getTranslation
        (position));
    }

    private void drawShadows(float delta) {
        shadowLight.begin(Vector3.Zero,
        perspectiveCamera.direction);
        batch.begin(shadowLight.getCamera());
        for (int x = 0; x < entities.size(); x++) {
            if (entities.get(x).getComponent(PlayerComponent.class)
            != null || entities.get(x).getComponent
            (EnemyComponent.class) != null) {
                ModelComponent mod =
                entities.get(x).getComponent(ModelComponent.class);
                if (isVisible(perspectiveCamera, mod.instance))
                batch.render(mod.instance);
            }
            if
            (entities.get(x).getComponent(AnimationComponent.class)
            != null & Settings.Paused == false)
            entities.get(x).getComponent(AnimationComponent.class)
            .update(delta);
        }
        batch.end();
```

```
            shadowLight.end();
        }
    }
```

Add a new Boolean method called `isVisible(...)` with `Camera` and `ModelInstance` as parameters. We want to compare where in the world the model is and check if the camera is looking at that point. For this task, the camera comes with a frustum instance that comes with a handy method called `PointInFrustum(...)` and takes a matrix.

Then, we will add our new method in the middle of the `for` iteration of the `drawShadows` method inside an `if` check, and that's it! If the model is inside the camera's vision, it will draw the shadow.

As you may have figured, this method needs improvement, for which the frustum has other methods; one, for example, is called `boundsInFrustum`. Can you see how to improve it now?

UI tweening

Games can use a lot of polishing in a lot of areas; one of those is UI tweening and customization. As mentioned earlier, Scene2D gives us a lot of flexibility in the user interface part of apps and one of those is UI tweening. Let's use a bit of this capability.

Let's open up the `MainMenuScreen` class and add the following code:

```
public class MainMenuScreen implements Screen {
    ...
    private void configureWidgers() {
        backgroundImage.setSize(Core.VIRTUAL_WIDTH,
        Core.VIRTUAL_HEIGHT);
        backgroundImage.setColor(1, 1, 1, 0);
        backgroundImage.addAction(Actions.fadeIn(0.65f));
        titleImage.setSize(620, 200);
        titleImage.setPosition(Core.VIRTUAL_WIDTH / 2 -
        titleImage.getWidth() / 2, Core.VIRTUAL_HEIGHT / 2);
        titleImage.setColor(1, 1, 1, 0);
        titleImage.addAction(new
        SequenceAction(Actions.delay(0.65f),
        Actions.fadeIn(0.75f)));
        playButton.setSize(128, 64);
        playButton.setPosition(Core.VIRTUAL_WIDTH / 2 -
        playButton.getWidth() / 2, Core.VIRTUAL_HEIGHT / 2 - 100);
        playButton.setColor(1, 1, 1, 0);
        playButton.addAction(new
```

```
SequenceAction(Actions.delay(0.65f),
Actions.fadeIn(0.75f)));
leaderboardsButton.setSize(128, 64);
leaderboardsButton.setPosition(Core.VIRTUAL_WIDTH / 2 -
playButton.getWidth() / 2, Core.VIRTUAL_HEIGHT / 2 - 170);
leaderboardsButton.setColor(1, 1, 1, 0);
leaderboardsButton.addAction(new
SequenceAction(Actions.delay(0.65f),
Actions.fadeIn(0.75f)));
quitButton.setSize(128, 64);
quitButton.setPosition(Core.VIRTUAL_WIDTH / 2 -
playButton.getWidth() / 2, Core.VIRTUAL_HEIGHT / 2 - 240);
quitButton.setColor(1, 1, 1, 0);
quitButton.addAction(new
SequenceAction(Actions.delay(0.65f),
Actions.fadeIn(0.75f)));
    ...
    }
}
```

We will take images and buttons and first set the colors to red, green, blue, and alpha (1, 1, 1, 0) to make them completely transparent, and then we will use a method called addAction(...) that all of them have, even though they are different classes, because they are all actors. For the background image, we will use Actions.fadeIn(...) and pass 0.65f, which means the fade-in will happen at a bit more than half a second. With those two lines of code, we will tell the actor to do the face in action, but you can do all kinds of actions, you just have to explore the classes a bit.

Now, for the other actors, we will also change the alpha color; but for the action, we will use a class called SequenceAction that gives us the option to add multiple animations and play them in a sequence. Now, we will use a method called delay(...) from the Actions class, then a comma, and then fadeIn(...) again. Then run the app and see how it works.

Now, open ScoreWidget and make a few additions and modifications, as shown in the following code:

```
public class ScoreWidget extends Actor {
    private Label label;
    private Container container;
    private int score;

    public ScoreWidget() {
        label = new Label("", Assets.skin);
        score = 0;
        container = new Container(label);
        container.setTransform(true);
```

```
            container.fill();
    }

    @Override
    public void act(float delta) {
        container.act(delta);
        if (PlayerComponent.score > score) {
            container.addAction(new
            SequenceAction(Actions.scaleBy(0.5f, 0.25f, 0.3f),
            Actions.scaleBy(-0.5f, -0.25f, 0.3f)));
        }
        score = PlayerComponent.score;
        label.setText("Score : " + PlayerComponent.score);
    }

    @Override
    public void draw(Batch batch, float parentAlpha) {
        container.draw(batch, parentAlpha);
    }

    @Override
    public void setPosition(float x, float y) {
        super.setPosition(x, y);
        container.setPosition(x, y);
    }

    @Override
    public void setSize(float width, float height) {
        super.setSize(width, height);
        container.setSize(width, height);
    }
}
```

Modifications are quite an amount on the class because in order to use a Label class with Actions, we will first need to add it to a Container class (even if the Label class lets you add Actions, they won't work on this version of LibGDX, at least).

We will want to make the score jump when it increases, so we will add a sequence action where we first scale it up and then down.

Take a look at all of the methods on the class as they have now replaced most of the label's positions.

Online leaderboards and the .NET API

We'd like to show a bit of the Internet connection capabilities of LibGDX and a great service to engage players—online leaderboards. For a game like ours that should be focused on score, this feature is a great addition.

A service called **dreamlo** (http://dreamlo.com/) lets us have a leaderboard in the cloud and in order to connect to it, we have specific and simple classes brought by LibGDX's awesomeness.

Let's open the LeaderboardsScreen class and make changes, as shown in the following code:

```
public class LeaderboardsScreen implements Screen {
    Core game;
    Stage stage;
    Image backgroundImage;
    TextButton backButton;
    Label label[];
    boolean loaded;

    public LeaderboardsScreen(Core game) {
        this.game = game;
        stage = new Stage(new FitViewport(Core.VIRTUAL_WIDTH,
        Core.VIRTUAL_HEIGHT));
        setWidgets();
        configureWidgers();
        setListeners();
        Gdx.input.setInputProcessor(stage);
    }

    private void setWidgets() {
        backgroundImage = new Image(new
        Texture(Gdx.files.internal("data/backgroundMN.png")));
        backButton = new TextButton("Back", Assets.skin);
        label = new Label[5];
        label[0] = new Label("Loading scores from online
        leaderborads...", Assets.skin);
        Settings.load(label);
    }

    private void configureWidgers() {
        backgroundImage.setSize(Core.VIRTUAL_WIDTH,
        Core.VIRTUAL_HEIGHT);
        backButton.setSize(128, 64);
        backButton.setPosition(Core.VIRTUAL_WIDTH -
        backButton.getWidth() - 5, 5);
```

```
        stage.addActor(backgroundImage);
        stage.addActor(backButton);

        label[0].setFontScale(3);
        label[0].setPosition(15, Core.VIRTUAL_HEIGHT -
        label[0].getHeight() - 25);
        stage.addActor(label[0]);
    }

    private void setListeners() {
        backButton.addListener(new ClickListener() {
            @Override
            public void clicked(InputEvent event, float x, float y) {
                game.setScreen(new MainMenuScreen(game));
            }
        });
    }

    @Override
    public void render(float delta) {
        /** Updates */
        stage.act(delta);
        updateLeaderboard();
        /** Draw */
        stage.draw();
    }

    public void updateLeaderboard() {
        if (label[1] != null && loaded == false) {
            loaded = true;
            int y = 0;
            for (int i = 0; i < label.length; i++) {
                label[i].setFontScale(3);
                label[i].setPosition(15, Core.VIRTUAL_HEIGHT -
                label[i].getHeight() - 25 - y);
                y += 96;
                stage.addActor(label[i]);
            }
        }
    }
}
...
}
```

We added a Boolean and changed a bit of the initialization on `setWidgets()` and added the `load(..)` method of `Settings` class that now takes the `label` array. Everything else stays the same.

Now, let's open the `Settings` class:

```
public class Settings {
    public static boolean Paused;
    public static boolean soundEnabled = true;
    public final static String file = ".spaceglad";
    private static final String leaderURL =
    "http://dreamlo.com/lb/PLfBGtHgG02wU0lSzVNrPAG0uQf3J3
    -UGzK1i7mXmmxA";
    private static final String request5 = "/pipe/5";

    public static void load(final Label[] leaderboardItems) {
        Net.HttpRequest requestBests = new
        Net.HttpRequest(Net.HttpMethods.GET);
        requestBests.setUrl(leaderURL + request5);
        Gdx.net.sendHttpRequest(requestBests, new
        Net.HttpResponseListener() {
            @Override
            public void handleHttpResponse(Net.HttpResponse
            httpResponse) {
                System.out.println(httpResponse);
                String string = new
                String(httpResponse.getResultAsString());
                String scores[] = string.split("\n");
                if (scores.length > 0)
                    for (int i = 0; i < scores.length; i++) {
                        String score[] = scores[i].split("\\|");
                        if (i == 0)
                          leaderboardItems[i].setText(String.valueOf
                          (Integer.valueOf(score[score.length - 1]) +
                          1) + ")" + score[0] + ": " + score[1]);
                        else
                          leaderboardItems[i] = new
                          Label(String.valueOf(Integer.valueOf
                          (score[score.length - 1]) + 1) + ")"
                          + score[0] + ": " + score[1],
                          Assets.skin);
                    }
            }

            @Override
            public void failed(Throwable t) {
                System.out.println(t);
            }
```

```
            @Override
            public void cancelled() {
                System.out.println("Cancel");
            }
        });
    }

    public static void load() {
        try {
            FileHandle filehandle = Gdx.files.external(file);
            String[] strings = filehandle.readString().split("\n");
            soundEnabled = Boolean.parseBoolean(strings[0]);
        } catch (Throwable e) {
        }
    }

    public static void save() {
        try {
            FileHandle filehandle = Gdx.files.external(file);
            filehandle.writeString(Boolean.toString(soundEnabled) +
            "\n", false);
        } catch (Throwable e) {
        }
    }

    public static void sendScore(int score) {
        Net.HttpRequest request = new Net.HttpRequest("GET");
        request.setUrl("http://dreamlo.com/lb/
        PLfBGtHgG02wU01SzVNrPAG0uQf3J3-UGzK1i7mXmmxA/add/" +
        "SpaceGladiator" + "/" + score);
        Gdx.net.sendHttpRequest(request, new
        Net.HttpResponseListener() {
            @Override
            public void handleHttpResponse(Net.HttpResponse
            httpResponse) {
            }

            @Override
            public void failed(Throwable t) {
            }

            @Override
            public void cancelled() {
            }
        });
    }
}
```

We now have a new string called `leaderUrl` that has our leaderboards URL in `dreamlo.com`, and another string called `request5` that adds to the URL occasionally (read dreamlo's leaderboard description). The new `load(...)` method takes a `label` array and starts using the .NET API: first, it instantiates a `Net.HttpRequest` method, setting the http method `Get`, and on the next line, setting the URL to our leaderboards plus the request of the first five scores. What it does next is it actually sends the request with a .NET API's static method, `Gdx.net.sendHttpRequest()`, and takes the request and a listener. Now, this listener is the one who will populate the `label` array once it receives the data.

The other method that has a substantial change is `sendScore(...)`; it's almost the same as `load(...)` but the URL changes to send scores.

Now, run the game and navigate to the leaderboards:

After a few seconds, you will see the scores appearing on the screen:

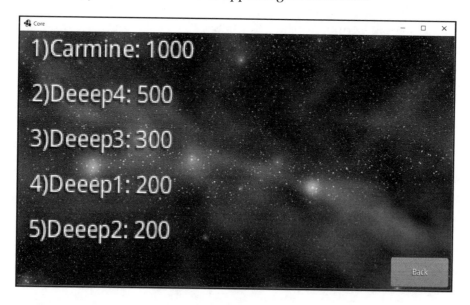

Analog sticks on mobile and platform recognition

The game runs on mobile without any problem on mid-end devices, and it should work fine on most devices too. However, our game isn't really suited to play on mobiles because of the input. We can fix that by adding analog sticks to the screens, as usual for a lot of games.

We'll create a new widget to handle this controller.

Let's fire up `GameUI.java`:

```java
public class GameUI {
    ...
    private ControllerWidget controllerWidget;

    public void setWidgets() {
        ...
        if (Gdx.app.getType() ==
        Application.ApplicationType.Android) controllerWidget = new
        ControllerWidget();
    }
```

```
    public void configureWidgets() {
        ...
        if (Gdx.app.getType() ==
        Application.ApplicationType.Android)
        controllerWidget.addToStage(stage);
    }
}
```

Addition to this class is a widget called `ControllerWidget`. It adds the sticks to the screen, but only if the platform running the app is mobile. We added the `Gdx.app.getType()` and then confirmed that it's on Android; you could do the same for all other platforms, of course. Instead of setting `stage.addActor(...)`, the widget will need its own method called `addToStage(...)`.

Now, let's create a widget in the `UI` package:

```
public class ControllerWidget {
    private static Touchpad movementPad;
    private static Touchpad watchPad;
    private static Vector2 movementVector;
    private static Vector2 watchVector;

    public ControllerWidget() {
        Touchpad.TouchpadStyle touchpadStyle = new
        Touchpad.TouchpadStyle();
        touchpadStyle.knob = new TextureRegionDrawable(new
        TextureRegion(new
        Texture(Gdx.files.internal("data/touchKnob.png"))));
        touchpadStyle.knob.setMinWidth(64);
        touchpadStyle.knob.setMinHeight(64);
        touchpadStyle.background = new TextureRegionDrawable(new
        TextureRegion(new
        Texture(Gdx.files.internal("data/touchBackground.png"))));
        touchpadStyle.background.setMinWidth(64);
        touchpadStyle.background.setMinHeight(64);

        movementPad = new Touchpad(10, touchpadStyle);
        watchPad = new Touchpad(10, touchpadStyle);

        movementPad.setColor(0.5f, 0.5f, 0.5f, 0.5f);
        watchPad.setColor(0.5f, 0.5f, 0.5f, 0.5f);

        movementVector = new Vector2(0, 0);
        watchVector = new Vector2(0, 0);
    }

    public void addToStage(Stage stage) {
```

```
        movementPad.setBounds(15, 15, 300, 300);
        watchPad.setBounds(stage.getWidth() - 315, 15, 300, 300);
        stage.addActor(movementPad);
        stage.addActor(watchPad);
    }

    public static Vector2 getMovementVector() {
        movementVector.set(movementPad.getKnobPercentX(),
        movementPad.getKnobPercentY());
        return movementVector;
    }

    public static Vector2 getWatchVector() {
        watchVector.set(watchPad.getKnobPercentX(),
        watchPad.getKnobPercentY());
        return watchVector;
    }
}
```

As simple as it can be, it uses a LibGDX class called `Touchpad`, which doesn't need an explanation of what it is for. It includes two of them, left for player movement and right for camera movement. And then, we have two `Vectors2` with their respective static methods to constantly check for positions in the `PlayerSystem`.

For the touchpads, we will need a `TouchpadStyle` class; it need textures, one for the touch knob field and one for the `background`. So, on the widget constructor, we instantiate the `TouchpadStyle` class first, then add the `knob` along with setting its minimum width and height, and then the `background` with its minimum width and height too. Just after that, we will instantiate the touchpads with a deadzone radius of 10 and the style. Then set their color to transparent and instantiate the vectors.

The `addToStage` method will implement the `stage.addActor` method, but first, it will set the bounds for the pads, they need x and y position, and width and height.

Now, to actually use the widget, we need a few modifications on the `PlayerSystem.class`:

```
    public class PlayerSystem extends EntitySystem implements EntityListener,
    InputProcessor {
        ...

        private void updateMovement(float delta) {
            if (Gdx.app.getType() ==
            Application.ApplicationType.Android) {
                deltaX = -ControllerWidget.getWatchVector().x * 1.5f;
```

```
        deltaY = ControllerWidget.getWatchVector().y * 1.5f;
    } else {
        deltaX = -Gdx.input.getDeltaX() * 0.5f;
        deltaY = -Gdx.input.getDeltaY() * 0.5f;
    }
    tmp.set(0, 0, 0);
    camera.rotate(camera.up, deltaX);
    tmp.set(camera.direction).crs(camera.up).nor();
    camera.direction.rotate(tmp, deltaY);
    tmp.set(0, 0, 0);
    characterComponent.characterDirection.set(-1, 0,
    0).rot(modelComponent.instance.transform).nor();
    characterComponent.walkDirection.set(0, 0, 0);
    if (Gdx.app.getType() ==
    Application.ApplicationType.Android) {
        if (ControllerWidget.getMovementVector().y > 0)
         characterComponent.walkDirection.add(camera.direction);
        if (ControllerWidget.getMovementVector().y < 0)
         characterComponent.walkDirection.sub(camera.direction);
        if (ControllerWidget.getMovementVector().x < 0)
         tmp.set(camera.direction).crs(camera.up).scl(-1);
        if (ControllerWidget.getMovementVector().x > 0)
         tmp.set(camera.direction).crs(camera.up);
        characterComponent.walkDirection.add(tmp);
        characterComponent.walkDirection.scl(10f * delta);
        characterComponent.characterController.setWalkDirection
        (characterComponent.walkDirection);
    } else {
        if (Gdx.input.isKeyPressed(Input.Keys.W))
         characterComponent.walkDirection.add(camera.direction);
        if (Gdx.input.isKeyPressed(Input.Keys.S))
         characterComponent.walkDirection.sub(camera.direction);
        if (Gdx.input.isKeyPressed(Input.Keys.A))
         tmp.set(camera.direction).crs(camera.up).scl(-1);
        if (Gdx.input.isKeyPressed(Input.Keys.D))
         tmp.set(camera.direction).crs(camera.up);
        characterComponent.walkDirection.add(tmp);
        characterComponent.walkDirection.scl(10f * delta);
        characterComponent.characterController
        .setWalkDirection(characterComponent.walkDirection);
    }
    ghost.set(0, 0, 0, 0);
    translation.set(0, 0, 0);
    translation = new Vector3();
    characterComponent.ghostObject.getWorldTransform(ghost);   //TODO
export this
    ghost.getTranslation(translation);
    modelComponent.instance.transform.set(translation.x,
```

```
                translation.y, translation.z, camera.direction.x,
                camera.direction.y, camera.direction.z, 0);
                camera.position.set(translation.x, translation.y,
                translation.z);
                camera.update(true);

            dome.getComponent(ModelComponent.class)
            .instance.transform.setToTranslation(translation.x,
            translation.y, translation.z);

            if (Gdx.input.isKeyPressed(Input.Keys.SPACE)) {
                // TODO change this back to 25
                characterComponent.characterController.setJumpSpeed(25);
                characterComponent.characterController.jump();
            }
            if (Gdx.input.justTouched()) fire();
        }
        ...
    }
```

The changes are on updateMovement() and they are small ones, but to avoid confusion, we'll leave the whole method pasted for you.

We will add a new if condition that checks again for the platform, and if it is Android, it will start reading our static vector methods of the widget.

This approach has a couple of problems because of the way we implemented the input back then. One problem is that every time we touch the screen, the gun will fire and the other is the implementation of the Jump button for mobile. A well designed UI interface can make a good controller on mobile for fire, jump, movement, and watching. We'll leave that task for you to explore.

Now, run it on mobile and see what it looks like:

Summary

In this chapter, you learned how to improve your app's performance and do basic polishing with publishing and making the game prettier for the public in mind. We also tested the game on a mobile and made specific blocks of code for different platforms, making different inputs on platforms without big changes.

In the next chapter, we will perform the closing steps to release the game to the public and talk about what's missing in the app that we created in this book.

7
Final Words

In this final chapter, we'll test our game on Android devices as well as desktops, and then deploy it. We'll also recognize when we are on a specific platform to activate the joystick, keyboard, or onscreen buttons.

In this chapter, we will cover the following topics:

- Deploying to a desktop
- Deploying to Android
- Gradle terminal use
- Troubleshooting common problems
- What's missing in our app/game
- Basic game design

Deploying to platforms

For the finishing touches of our game, we will deploy the application; for this, LibGDX comes with handy methods. Open the terminal in IntelliJ with *Alt + F12* or navigate to the top-left side on **View** | **Tool Windows** | **Terminal**.

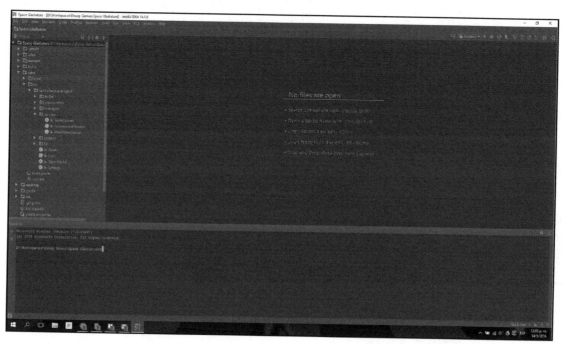

Running and deploying on desktop

To run on the desktop, we can use (other than the buttons on IntelliJ) `gradlew desktop:run`. Keep in mind that the running directory will be the in Android project's `asset` folder.

To deploy, we will use `gradlew desktop:dist` in the terminal. It creates a JAR file in the `desktop/build/libs/` folder. It can be run by double-clicking or in the terminal by using `java -jar jar-file-name.jar`. Though the operating system needs JVM to run a file, it will work on Windows, Linux, and Mac OS X.

Running and deploying on Android

To run on Android, we will write and run `gradlew android:installDebug android:run` in the terminal.

To deploy on Android, we will write and run `gradlew android:assembleRelease` in the terminal. This creates an unsigned APK file in the `android/build/outputs/apk` folder, which can be used on Android devices that have the installation from unknown sources enabled. This APK file is only meant for debugging purposes. In order to publish the app in the Play Store and be distributed to the world, you'll need the APK file signed. To sign it, go to the top nav bar in IntelliJ and navigate to **Build | Generate Signed APK**; it will ask for a keystore that you can create there.

Troubleshooting common problems

During development, we'll run into different kinds of problems. We will address a few common ones.

Gradle

When Gradle tasks fail and the error is not clear enough, you can try adding `--debug` to the tasks to expand the error description: for example, `gradlew desktop:dist --debug`.

A command that is useful for fixes is `gradlew clean`. You'll use this command often.

Antivirus

It's confirmed that AVG Antivirus causes `gradlew desktop:dist` to fail. Add an exception to the antivirus.

IntelliJ

Sometimes, IDEs fail randomly; a solution that we found on IntelliJ IDEA is reindexing. You can click on **File | Invalidate Caches / Restart...** for reindexing.

When software updates are available, you might need to reindex and load everything again, which means using `gradlew clean` too.

What's missing from our game?

There are a lot of things that we can include and improve in our apps to make our game more appealing for players; listed are some points that you can keep in mind while creating your own game.

More platforms

We know that LibGDX supports several platforms, such as desktop, Android, iPhone, HTML, and even OUYA. Every platform has its own tricks and as seen in the *Analog sticks on mobile and platform recognition* of `Chapter 6`, *Spicing Up the Game*, sometimes we also need to write specific code. For this, there's options such as interfaces between platforms that load classes depending on the platform where the app is being run (see mobile ads for LibGDX). Other things that can limit development on platforms are, for example, to deploy an iPhone, you need to use Mac OS X with XCode; and for our specific purpose, Bullet Physics is not available on HTML.

You may want to consider deploying to several platforms at the same time. Taken directly from `https://li bgdx.badlogicgames.com/features.html` in May 2016, you have:

Cross-Platform

A single API to target:
- Windows
- Linux
- Mac OS X
- Android (2.2+)
- BlackBerry
- iOS
- Java Applet (requires JVM to be installed)
- Javascript/WebGL (Chrome, Safari, Opera, Firefox, IE via **Google Chrome Frame**)

Loading screen and loading feature

An important feature is to show the player the app hasn't frozen. Some desktops and mobile devices might not load models fast, and we can't expect our players to be patient.

There are nice tricks and methods from the `AssetManager` class that helps us get a simpler and faster structure to handle our assets.

Here's an example of a loading screen made with LibGDX:

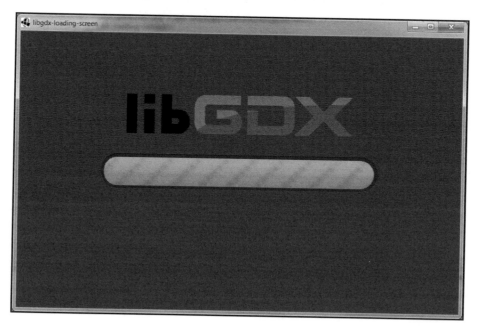

About section

We can add a section that contains information regarding contact pages, e-mails, the app version, and the people involved so that it is easier for the audience to reach out to you in case they have any concerns or feedback about the game.

Splash screen

The splash screen is also referred to as a boot screen, boot skin, or welcome screen—a screen that gives information about the developer and publisher, most likely does the actual loading of the app and can do some other things, such as starting the immersion of players to the game's ambience.

A beautiful splash screen from **Monument Valley** looks like a book cover:

UI customization and screen transitions

These aspects are a big part of making the game appealing as well as a big part of the polishing stage of development. We can make custom buttons, custom font, more tweenings, and screen transitions between states (main menu to game, for example). It adds a professional and unique look, smoothens the human eye transitions, and gives you a style of your own.

A big dialog window or small dialog window with yes and no buttons, health bars, and so on, are examples of a custom UI on a game made by Deeep Games with LibGDX.

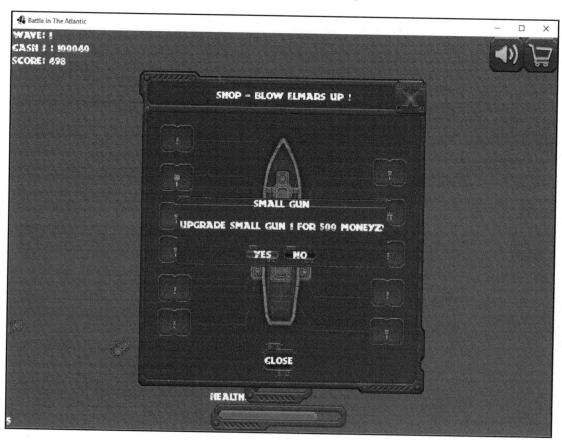

Game design

Game design is arguably one of the most important aspects of a game. To avoid filling pages and pages of content, and also save development time, the book focuses on actually showing how to program a 3D game as well as important, basic, aspects to know and keep in mind for this kind of development. However, game design can take up to months or years of polishing on its own. It is recommended that you take your time to focus on aspects you may want to improve, such as fun, challenge, immersion, atmosphere, and a million other aspects that could be important to you and your demographics. There are lots of great books on it.

In any case, we are not completely off in game design. The development stages shown in this book are very effective and there are some simple game design approaches. We covered the following steps:

- **Idea**: We get to see a bit of what we want to achieve.
- **Prototype**: We will turn our idea into something tangible, study development efforts, and study game design roads, looping as much as we want into ideas and concepts.
- **Full game stage**: We will implement aspects such as final artwork, concepts, story, and polishing the gameplay.
- **Extras or polishing stage**: We will make it look professional, polish the artwork, and take care of polishing details such as adding an "About" section and splash screens.

All these steps come with the amount of iterations that you need to improve them. Iterations are what we skipped the most in this book, and they are vital in game design.

Attack system

An attack system is one aspect that can be of great benefit to include. For simplicity reasons, and because we did something very similar with shooting in the `PlayerSystem` class, we omitted this feature; however, with the information given, it should be enough to develop a system.

Basically, the idea was to use a `Ray` class, just like shooting in the `PlayerSystem`, which would be thrown a few moments before the enemy attack animation finishes (just when the claw is touching the player) and check whether the player is in front of it and close enough, then make the player take damage. The idea is the same as shooting, but it needs a different calculation as we will do it from the enemy's perspective.

Shaders and shadows across all platforms

We implemented shadows in a way simple enough for everyone to actually make it work, but there is much to learn in order to make it work on all sides, and this includes shaders. A shader's capability is much broader than just shadows; however, this is also a very broad and advanced topic.

The following image is an example of a game with some good work on shaders:

Shooting lasers

Shooting lasers is another great feature that can be complex and broad to cover. It can be made of models and/or shaders, particles, and lighting. It's just a matter of getting into it and exploring the possibilities.

Positional audio

Audio is another feature that can be of great benefit in a 3D environment to give a sense of immersion. We will need a system to make use of the audio API.

Publishing

No piece of art is complete without the world seeing it, and, in our case, playing it as well. There's a bunch of markets and communities where we can share our work and deploy LibGDX, such as Steam, Play Store, App Store, forums, and communities. Every market and community has its own rules and scopes, which we can use, to get a huge benefit to improve a lot of areas in the app.

Ads

Ads are no less important for developers to know how to implement. After all, there are people and companies that live from game development and their free games. It is out of the scope of this book to get into this subject, but it does not hurt to let you know that LibGDX can implement on a variety of platforms and APIs and different kinds of ads too (fullscreen ads, banners, and so on).

The possibilities for platforms vary. We can find backends shared by developers in LibGDX's forum or we can create our own. As a start, by interfacing on platform-specific code we can find implementations of the following:

- **AdMob (Android)**: Checkout `https://www.google.es/admob/`
- **AdSense (HTML)**: Available at `https://www.google.com/adsense`
- **iAds (iPhone)**: Located at `http://advertising.apple.com/`

Social networks

We can always add a bit of networking for people to connect and share.

The possibilities are as follows:

- **Facebook**: This app sends scores, shares games, and so on. It depends on how you want to use it. There's currently a backend build for it at `https://github.com/TomGrill/gdx-facebook`, and there might be a lot more.
- **Google Play Services**: This app shares social leaderboards, achievements, multiplayers, cloud saves, and lots more.
- **Twitter**: This app shares basic things. It also depends on how you want to use it. Additionally, you will need to be a Twitter developer to implement it.

Summary

In this chapter, we went over the process of preparing to deploy our app, run from the terminal using Gradle, troubleshoot common problems, and whatever areas we have left in the game.

We hope you learned enough to be comfortable with 3D and create simple games and also know what direction to head in to produce more professional games with this awesome tool.

Index

collision worlds 40

C

camera techniques 15, 16
collision bounds
  modifying 159
collision detection 37
collision-related components
  implementing 38
collisions
  adding 36
common problems, troubleshooting
  about 209
  AVG Antivirus 210
  Gradle task failure 210
  IDE failure 210
controls
  setting up, for gun animation 130, 131, 132,
    134, 135
crosshair
  adding 69
cube
  drawing 16, 17, 18, 19, 20

D

death animation 169
default skin, for Scene2D 65
desktop
  application, deploying on 208, 209
  application, running on 208, 209
directional shadow
  adding, with light 176
dreamlo
  reference 195

E

edges 98
emitter properties 182, 183
enemies
  adding 53
enemy collision 56, 59
enemy component 53
enemy model
  about 161
  performance improvements 189

enemy system 54, 56
Entity Management System 33

F

Facebook
  about 217
  reference 217
faces 98
Fbx-Conv
  command-line usage 144
  downloading 144
  flags 145
  options 145
  reference 144
Flame 180
frustum culling 191

G

game asset pipeline, Blender
  about 93
  modeling 94, 95, 96, 98, 99, 100, 102, 104,
    105, 106, 107, 108, 109, 110, 112, 113, 114,
    115, 116
  texturing 124, 125, 126, 127, 128, 130
  UV mapping 116, 117, 118, 119, 120, 121,
    122, 123
game design approaches
  full game stage 215
  idea 215
  prototype 215
game over widget
  creating 76, 78
game screen
  implementing 30, 31
game world
  about 31, 32
  creating 27
  floor, creating 31
  structure, creating 28, 29, 30
  visuals, adding 33
game
  pausing 72, 75
GLSL 176
Google Play Services 217
Google Web Toolkit (GWT) 11